THE UPDATED

VERMONT

TRAVEL GUIDE IN 2023

A simple Guide on How Travelers can Explore this Enchanting State. Everything You Need to Know to Make the Most Out of Your Trip

D1714745

OPEN PLANET

TABLE OF CONTENT

CHAPTER NINE

THE UPDATED VERMONT TRAVEL GUIDE IN 2023

INTRODUCTION

Greetings from the Green Mountain State, Vermont! For anybody who enjoys natural beauty, outdoor activity, and a relaxed way of life, Vermont is a must-visit location with its rolling hills, charming villages, and active cultural environment.

This travel manual will enable you to get the most out of your time in Vermont whether you're a frequent traveler or a first-time visitor. The top sights, events, and secret spots that highlight Vermont's distinctive character have been culled from our extensive search of the state.

Vermont has plenty to offer everyone, from the charming communities of Woodstock and Stowe to the vibrant city of Burlington. Explore the state's rich history and culture, take a scenic drive along Route 100, go on a hike through the Green Mountains, or try some artisan cheese or craft beer.

Our guidebook is crammed with insider information, thorough maps, and suggestions from people who live there and know Vermont the best. We provide helpful suggestions on how to move around, stay in hotels, and eat, whether you're organizing a weekend trip or a longer holiday.

So come along and find out why Vermont is one of the nation's favorite states. We promise that you'll fall in love with its unmatched natural beauty, endearing residents, and distinctive personality. Travel safely!

CHAPTER ONE

Introduction to Vermont

Brief History & Geography

In the northeastern part of the country is the state of Vermont. By population, it is the sixth-smallest state, and by land area, it is the second-smallest. Vermont, despite its modest size, has a long and varied history that has greatly influenced the state's topography, economy, and culture. We will thoroughly examine Vermont's geography and history in this chapter.

Geography

The states of New York to the west, New Hampshire to the east, and Massachusetts to the south border Vermont, which is located in the New England region of the country. With a population of about 624,000, the state has a total area of 9,616 square miles. Rolling hills, forests, and mountains make up Vermont's landscape, with the Green Mountains cutting through the state's middle from north to south. Mount Mansfield, which rises 4,393 feet above sea level, is Vermont's tallest peak.

The terrain of Vermont has greatly influenced the state's economy and culture. The state's plentiful forests have helped it become a center for the timber industry, and its rich soils have long supported agriculture. Winter sports enthusiasts frequently travel to the state because of its many mountains and ski areas.

History

The history of Vermont dates back long before any European people arrived. Numerous Native American tribes, such as the Abenaki, Mohawk, and Algonquin, lived in the area and utilized it for agriculture, hunting, and fishing.

Samuel de Champlain, a French explorer who landed in the area in 1609, was the first European to explore Vermont. However, European settlers did not start building long-term settlements in Vermont until the middle of the 18th century. The majority of these settlers were of English and Dutch descent, and they immediately set up farms and started to clear the area for farming.

Vermont became the first area in what would eventually become the United States to declare itself an independent republic in 1777. The state didn't become a part of the Union until 1791 when it was admitted as the fourteenth state. Vermont contributed significantly to the Union's cause during the American Civil War by providing thousands of soldiers to battle.

Vermont underwent substantial changes during the 19th and 20th centuries as its economy changed from one based on agriculture to one based on industry. The expansion of the lumber and paper industries was spurred by the state's plentiful natural resources, notably water power, and timber. The state also developed into a center for manufacturing, with businesses producing machinery, textiles, and other products.

The state's natural beauty and recreational opportunities drew tourists from all over the world in the 20th century, which caused Vermont's economy to move toward services and tourism. The economy of Vermont today is varied, encompassing sectors like sophisticated manufacturing, technology, and the tourist and hospitality industries.

Vermont's history, geography, and distinctive fusion of rural and urban elements all have an impact on the state's culture. Many Vermonters value independence and self-sufficiency, and the state has a long history of individuality, self-reliance, and communal involvement. Additionally, Vermont is renowned for its liberal politics and social activism, frequently leading movements for human rights, environmental protection, and social justice.

Farming, logging, and maple sugaring are just a few of the ancient crafts and industries that may be found in Vermont's rural areas. The state is renowned for the creation of artisanal foods and drinks, with local farmers, bakers, brewers, and cheese makers turning out some of the best goods in the nation.

The history of Vermont extends back to the time when many Native American tribes called the region home during the pre-Columbian era. The establishment of permanent communities and the clearing of land for agriculture were prompted by the advent of European settlers in the middle of the 18th century. In 1777, Vermont proclaimed itself an independent republic, and in 1791, it was accepted as the 14th state of the Union. Vermont was crucial to the Union's cause during the American Civil War.

Vermont's economy underwent substantial changes during the 19th and 20th centuries as it changed from an agrarian to an industrialized economy. The expansion of the lumber and paper industries was spurred by the state's plentiful natural resources, notably water power, and timber. The state also developed into a center for manufacturing, with businesses producing machinery, textiles, and other products. The economy of Vermont today is varied, encompassing sectors like sophisticated manufacturing, technology, and the tourist and hospitality industries.

The history, geography, and distinctive fusion of rural and urban elements in Vermont all affect its culture. Many Vermonters value independence and self-sufficiency, and the state has a long history of individuality, self-reliance, and communal involvement. Additionally, Vermont is renowned for its liberal politics and social activism, frequently leading movements for human rights, environmental protection, and social justice.

The geography and history of Vermont have contributed significantly to the development of its economy and culture. For generations, agriculture and other industries have been sustained by the country's abounding natural resources, which include fertile soils and ample timber. Traditional crafts and industries are found in Vermont's rural areas, while industry, technology, and tourism are concentrated in the state's cities and towns. Self-reliance, independence, and social action define Vermont's culture, which makes it distinct and dynamic.

Weather & Seasons

The weather and seasons are among the most crucial elements that affect the experience of visiting Vermont. This section will go over the many seasons in Vermont, typical weather patterns, and the best ways to dress for each one.

Spring

Typically, spring in Vermont lasts from March to May. The weather can be erratic at this time of year, with lows below zero and highs in the mid-sixties. In March, snow is still common, so tourists should dress for the cold and the humidity.

The temperature gradually warms up as spring goes on, and Vermont's scenery changes into a verdant paradise. The fauna gets more active when the trees begin to blossom and the flowers begin to bloom. It's the ideal time of year to visit one of Vermont's many state parks to take in the beauty and fresh air, like Green Mountain National Forest.

Summer

The most popular time of year for tourists to visit Vermont is during the summer, which lasts from June to August. With temperatures averaging in the mid-70s, this time of year is typically warm. However, especially in July and August, it's not unusual for temperatures to rise into the 80s or even 90s.

Throughout the summer, visitors can engage in a wide range of outdoor activities. While the state's mountains offer fantastic opportunities for hiking and mountain biking, Vermont's lakes and rivers are ideal for swimming, boating, and fishing. Visit Vermont's various small towns and villages over the summer to experience the cuisine and crafts made there, take part in fairs and festivals, and take in live theater and musical events.

Fall

One of the most stunning seasons of the year in Vermont is fall. The season is distinguished by its beautiful leaves and crisp, chilly air, and it normally lasts from September to November. The average temperature during this season is in the mid-fifties, but there is a lot of variation, especially around October.

Visitors from all over the world travel to Vermont to view the state's breathtaking autumnal colors because of the state's famed fall foliage. Although the exact date can change from year to year, mid-October is typically the best time to view the foliage. Visitors can take in the breathtaking vistas by taking scenic drives, hiking paths, or even hot air balloon rides.

Winter

Although Vermont's winters can be difficult, they are also a magical time of year. The weather is chilly and snowy during the season, which normally lasts from December to February. Below-freezing temperatures are possible, and snowstorms are frequent.

There are plenty of wintertime activities in Vermont, despite the chilly weather and snow. The state is well-known for its world-class skiing and snowboarding at ski resorts like Stowe, Killington, and Stratton. Along with other outdoor activities like snowshoeing, cross-country skiing, and ice skating, visitors can also engage in indoor pursuits like touring museums and art galleries.

Getting Ready for the Weather

Visitors to Vermont should be ready for the weather at all times, regardless of the season. It's crucial to bring layers of clothing because daytime temperatures might vary greatly. Rain can fall at any time of the year, so visitors should carry rain gear. Visitors should pack warm clothes, such as hats, gloves, and boots, to protect themselves from the cold and snow during the winter.

Before visiting Vermont, especially in the winter, it's a good idea to check the weather forecast. Snowstorms can result in airline cancellations and road closures, so travelers should make adequate plans and have a fallback in place in case of bad weather.

The weather is always a consideration while traveling to Vermont, regardless of the time of year. To get the most out of your stay, it's crucial to be organized and plan beforehand. Visitors may take advantage of everything Vermont has to offer, regardless of the weather, with the appropriate attire, equipment, and understanding of the weather patterns.

Visitors should take the time to learn about Vermont's distinctive customs and traditions in addition to dressing for the weather. In Vermont, there is constantly something new to learn about and explore, from the manufacture of maple syrup to the state's rich history and culture.

Vermont has plenty to offer everyone, whether you're a history buff, an outdoor enthusiast, or a fan of nature. Vermont is a state that will leave a lasting impact on everyone who visits thanks to its breathtaking landscapes, warm residents, and inviting communities.

CHAPTER TWO

Planning Your Trip

Best Time to Visit Vermont

Travelers from throughout the world frequently visit Vermont. However, it's critical to understand the ideal time to visit Vermont before making travel arrangements. The ideal time to visit Vermont may change based on your interests and preferences. To assist you in planning your journey, we will examine the many seasons and occasions in Vermont in this section.

the autumn (September to November)

In Vermont, fall is without a doubt the most well-liked season, and with good reason. The state is transformed into a bright work of art by the changing leaves, with stunning reds, oranges, and yellows. Late September or early October is typically when the fall foliage is at its best, however, this might change from year to year depending on the weather. To avoid missing the busy season, it is crucial to organize your vacation in advance.

Apple picking, pumpkin carving, and corn mazes are among fall activities. There are many apple orchards in Vermont, and you can tour one while sampling apple pies and fresh apple cider. If you are traveling with children, be sure to spend the day having fun at a corn maze or pumpkin farm.

(December to February) Winter

The best spot to be if you enjoy winter sports is Vermont. Vermont is a winter wonderland for skiers and snowboarders, home to some of the top ski resorts in the nation, including Stowe Mountain Resort, Killington Ski Resort, and Okemo Mountain Resort. In Vermont, the winter skiing season typically begins in late November and lasts through early April.

In addition to skiing and snowboarding, Vermont also provides a wide range of other winter sports, such as sledding, ice fishing, and snowshoeing. Book a stay in a log cabin and sip hot cocoa by the fire if you want a comfortable winter experience.

(March to May) spring

Vermont's spring is a transitional season, but it may still be a fantastic time to travel there. A beautiful scene is created as the snow begins to melt and the trees blossom. The spring is the best time to travel to Vermont if you enjoy maple syrup. The season for sugaring officially begins in March, and you may visit a sugarhouse to learn more about how maple syrup is made.

Given that the weather is beginning to warm up, spring is also a great time to go biking and hiking. A well-liked hiking route for nature enthusiasts is the Long Trail, which traverses Vermont. Bring your raincoat with you; spring in Vermont can be wet.

Summer (June through August)

In Vermont, summer is a season for outdoor activities, celebrations, and farm-to-table cuisine. There are lots of options for hiking, biking, kayaking, and swimming because of the pleasant weather and long days. Lake Champlain, one of the many lakes and rivers in Vermont, is a popular spot for boating and fishing.

The Vermont Maple Festival, the Strolling of the Heifers, and the Vermont Brewers Festival are all held during the summer in Vermont. The best of

Vermont's culture, cuisine, and beverages are highlighted during these events.

Your interests and choices will determine when is the best time to visit Vermont. September to November is the ideal time to travel if you enjoy the fall scenery. While spring is the ideal time for outdoor activities like tasting maple syrup, winter is ideal for skiing and snowboarding. Festivals and outdoor activities are more popular in the summer. Vermont has something for everyone, no matter the time of year. To guarantee you get the most out of your trip to this stunning state, plan beforehand.

Getting to Vermont

If you are planning a trip to Vermont, you'll need to know how to get there. In this section, we'll explore the various ways to get to Vermont, including airports, train stations, and highways.

Airports:

Vermont has two primary airports: Burlington International Airport (BTV) and Rutland Southern Vermont Regional Airport (RUT). Both airports offer commercial flights and provide easy access to the state's many attractions.

Burlington International Airport (BTV):

Burlington International Airport (BTV) is located in the city of South Burlington, just three miles from downtown Burlington. Several prominent airlines such as American Airlines, Delta Air Lines, JetBlue Airways, and United Airlines offer their services at the airport. The airport offers nonstop flights to many major cities, including New York, Boston, Washington, D.C., and Chicago.

Rutland Southern Vermont Regional Airport (RUT):

Rutland Southern Vermont Regional Airport (RUT) is located in the city of Rutland, about 20 miles from the ski resorts of Killington and Pico Mountain. Cape Air provides daily flights to Boston's Logan International Airport, serving the airport.

Train Stations:

If you prefer to travel by train, Amtrak's Ethan Allen Express and Vermonter lines provide service to Vermont.

Ethan Allen Express:

The Ethan Allen Express provides service from New York City's Penn Station to Rutland, Vermont. The train stops in several cities along the way, including Yonkers, Croton-Harmon, Poughkeepsie, and Albany-Rensselaer. The trip takes about six hours.

Vermonter:

The Vermonter provides service from Washington, D.C., to St. Albans, Vermont. The train stops in several cities along the way, including Philadelphia, New York City, Hartford, and Springfield. The trip takes about 13 hours.

Highways:

Vermont is easily accessible by car, with several major highways passing through the state.

Interstate 89 (I-89):

Interstate 89 runs north-south through Vermont, connecting the cities of Burlington and Montpelier. The highway also provides access to several ski resorts, including Stowe, Sugarbush, and Mad River Glen.

Interstate 91 (I-91):

Interstate 91 runs north-south through Vermont's eastern border, connecting the cities of Brattleboro and St. Johnsbury. The highway provides access to several attractions, including the Quechee Gorge and the St. Johnsbury Athenaeum.

US Route 7 (US-7):

US Route 7 runs north-south through western Vermont, connecting the cities of Bennington and Burlington. The highway provides access to several attractions, including the Bennington Battle Monument and the Shelburne Museum.

US Route 4 (US-4):

US Route 4 runs east-west through central Vermont, connecting the cities of Rutland and White River Junction. The highway provides access to several attractions, including the Quechee Gorge and the Vermont Institute of Natural Science.

Vermont is a beautiful state with many attractions, and there are several ways to get there. Whether you prefer to fly, take the train, or drive, there are plenty of options to choose from. Burlington International Airport and Rutland Southern Vermont Regional Airport provide easy access to the state's many attractions. The Ethan Allen Express and Vermonter train lines provide a scenic way to travel to Vermont. If you prefer to drive, Interstate 89, Interstate 91, US Route

Where to Stay

There are lots of wonderful options for lodging in Vermont, whether you're planning a weekend trip there or a longer stay. Vermont provides a wide selection of accommodations for any traveler, from welcoming bed and breakfasts to opulent resorts.

Hotels: There are several hotels in Vermont, ranging from high-end resorts to those that are more reasonably priced. Popular hotel chains like Hilton, Marriott, and Sheraton may be found in bigger cities like Burlington and Montpelier. These hotels frequently provide extras like on-site dining establishments, exercise centers, and swimming pools. Consider staying at one of Vermont's boutique hotels for a more distinctive experience. These more intimate lodgings provide a more individualized experience and frequently have distinctive qualities like picturesque vistas or old-world architecture.

The Essex, a well-known boutique hotel in Vermont, is situated near Essex Junction. With facilities like a full-service spa, farm-to-table dining, and access to surrounding hiking and biking trails, this hotel combines rustic charm with modern conveniences.

The Stowe Mountain Lodge is an excellent option for people seeking a luxurious experience. This hotel boasts a full-service spa, fitness center, and heated outdoor pool in addition to ski-in/ski-out access to the mountain.

Motels: These are a wonderful option if you're looking for something more reasonably priced. There are several individually owned motels in Vermont, many of which provide a warm and welcoming atmosphere. Motels in Vermont are a practical option for vacationers because many of them are close to well-known tourist attractions.

The Sunset Motor Inn, which is situated near Morrisville, is a well-liked motel in Vermont. This motel provides reasonably priced accommodations in tidy, comfortable rooms. The Ben and Jerry's Factory and the Stowe Ski Resort are only a couple of the well-known attractions close to the Sunset Motor Inn.

There are many different types of resorts to select from, however, Vermont is well renowned for its ski resorts. Vermont offers a wide range of lodging alternatives, whether you're seeking a romantic weekend or a family-friendly resort.

For families, the Woodstock Inn and Resort is a well-liked option. A kids' club and a game area are just a couple of the kid-friendly activities available at this resort. There are numerous eating options, a full-service spa, and a fitness facility at the Woodstock Inn and Resort.

Visit Twin Farms in Barnard for a more passionate encounter. This all-inclusive resort provides opulent lodging, fine dining, and a variety of activities. Twin Farms is situated on 300 acres of private land and gives visitors access to the nearby fields and woodlands.

Bed & Breakfasts: Vermont is home to a variety of attractive bed and breakfasts that provide a warm and welcoming environment. Many bed and breakfasts in Vermont are housed in old buildings, providing a fascinating look into the state's past.

The Inn at Shelburne Farms in Shelburne is a well-known bed and breakfast in Vermont. This inn boasts breathtaking views of Lake Champlain and is situated on a 1,400-acre working farm. Along with farm-to-table dining, The Inn at Shelburne Farms provides a range of outdoor activities, such as biking and hiking.

The Rabbit Hill Inn, which is situated in Lower Waterford, is yet another well-liked option. This bed & breakfast provides warm accommodations, fine food, and quick access to local sights like the White Mountains.

Campgrounds: Camping is a fantastic alternative for individuals who want to discover Vermont's natural beauty. There are various campgrounds in Vermont, ranging from RV parks to basic campsites.

The Green Mountain Family Campground, which is situated in Bristol, is a well-known campground in Vermont. This campsite provides tent and RV camping spaces as well as a number of facilities, like a pool and playground. Additionally, the Green Mountain Family Campground is close to well-liked biking and hiking routes.

The Lake Champagne Campground near Randolph Center is yet another fantastic place to camp. This campground is located next to a lovely lake and provides a range of activities, such as swimming, boating, and fishing. Families will love the Lake Champagne Campground since it features a playground and a game room.

In addition to these campgrounds, Vermont offers a wide variety of other possibilities. There are some campgrounds inside state parks, providing quick access to hiking trails and other outdoor pursuits. Others are situated close to well-known sites like the Quechee Gorge or the Vermont Teddy Bear Factory.

Overall, Vermont has a large selection of lodging choices. You're likely to discover something that suits your interests and price range, whether you're looking for an opulent resort or a basic campground. So begin making travel arrangements for Vermont right away and be ready to enjoy everything that this lovely state has to offer.

Transportation Rental

There are several scenic drives and biking routes in Vermont, a state known for its breathtaking natural beauty. Renting a vehicle, bike, or other form of transportation in Vermont is a terrific choice whether you want to explore the countryside or just need a dependable way to get around.

Vehicle Rental in Vermont

Those who prefer to explore Vermont at their own pace may find it helpful to rent a car. The state's major airports, as well as rental car companies in bigger towns and cities, all offer rental cars. There are rental car agencies all around the state, including many major chains like Avis, Enterprise, and Hertz as well as regional ones like Vermont Car Rentals.

There are a few things to consider when renting a car in Vermont. Check the age limitations set forth by the rental car business first. Some firms will rent to drivers as young as 21, however, the majority of rental car companies demand drivers to be at least 25 years old. Ask about insurance coverage as well because most rental car businesses provide extra insurance plans that may provide coverage beyond what your own auto insurance policy may provide.

One thing to bear in mind when driving in Vermont is that, especially in rural areas, the state's roadways can be congested and meandering. Renting an automobile with four-wheel drive or all-wheel drive, which can offer superior traction on steep hills and bad weather, maybe a smart idea if you are not accustomed to driving in these situations.

Bike rental in Vermont

There are many beautiful bike paths in Vermont, including the well-known Lake Champlain Bikeway, which encircles the lake's shoreline for more than 200 miles. The state's natural beauty may be explored on a bike, and many rental businesses provide both road bikes and mountain bikes.

It's crucial to select the best kind of bike for your needs while renting a bike in Vermont. A road bike or hybrid bike may be your best bet if you intend to ride on paved roads and bike paths. A mountain bike would be a better option if you intend to explore parts of the state's rougher terrain, such as the mountain biking paths in the Green Mountains.

Ask about renting helmets as well as other equipment like lights, locks, and repair kits. A wonderful approach to learning about the neighborhood bike trails is to take advantage of the many bike rental companies' guided tours and maps of the area.

Renting Other Vehicles in Vermont

There are several choices in Vermont if you're seeking a more unusual form of transportation. Renting a scooter or motorcycle is a common choice. The state's winding back roads and picturesque byways can be explored in great detail using this method. However, bear in mind that possessing a motorcycle license is typically a requirement in order to rent a motorcycle.

Renting a kayak or canoe is an additional choice. Renting a kayak or canoe can be a terrific way to explore the beautiful rivers and lakes that Vermont is home to. Make sure to enquire about any necessary permits as well as safety gear, such as life jackets and paddles.

Finally, there are several businesses that provide horse-drawn carriage rides for people looking for a genuinely distinctive experience. The state's rural landscapes and historical landmarks can be explored in great detail with this method. However, bear in mind that weather restrictions and potential scheduling requirements may apply to horse-drawn carriage rides.

Do your homework and pick a reputed rental business that provides dependable vehicles and equipment before renting any kind of vehicle in

Vermont. Additionally, be aware of any age limitations, insurance prerequisites, and safety regulations related to the rental.

In Vermont, renting a car, bike, or other mode of transportation is a terrific opportunity to experience the region's natural splendor at your own pace. There are options available to meet any traveler's preferences, whether you decide to hire a car for the ultimate road trip, a bike to explore the state's bike paths or a special mode of transportation like a motorcycle or horse-drawn carriage.

Tips for Traveling with Kids, Pet or Disabled People

Any vacation can be made more complicated by traveling with children, animals, or people with disabilities, but with the right planning and preparation, it can also be a positive experience for everyone involved. Families and those with special needs will enjoy Vermont's breathtaking natural beauty and family-friendly attractions. We'll provide some advice in this area on how to make the most of your trip to Vermont, whether you're taking children, pets, or persons with disabilities.

Travel with children

Taking a trip with children can be exciting and difficult, but with some planning, you can make the experience more pleasant. Here are some recommendations for families visiting Vermont:

Consider your children when creating your itinerary: When selecting activities and attractions, take into account their interests and level of energy. Family-friendly activities in Vermont include swimming, hiking, and visiting farms and museums.

Pack sensibly: Bring plenty of snacks, water, and amusements like movies, games, and novels. Additionally, be sure to pack clothing appropriate for the environment and any outdoor activities.

Remain in a family-friendly hotel: Look for lodgings like hotels, resorts, or vacation homes that have facilities for kids like playgrounds, swimming pools, and scheduled activities.

Use a carrier or stroller: A stroller or child carrier might make it simpler to go around and take in Vermont's natural beauty if you have young children.

Take breaks: Children might become drained and irritable, so be sure to give them opportunities to relax and refuel throughout the day.

Taking Pets on Vacation

Vermont is a popular destination for pet owners because of its pet-friendly lodging and outdoor activities. Traveling with pets, however, necessitates additional planning and preparation. Here are some pointers about bringing your pet on a trip to Vermont:

Look for pet-friendly hotels: Make sure to do your research and reserve pet-friendly lodging in advance because not all hotels, vacation rentals, or campsites accept pets.

Pet supplies to bring: Bring food, water, toys, bedding, and any required prescriptions for your pet. Pack a leash, trash bags, and a pet first aid kit as well.

Plan activities that are pet-friendly: Outdoor activities that are dog-friendly in Vermont include hiking, swimming, and visiting dog parks. Plan carefully though, as some sites, like museums or restaurants, could not allow pets.

Pet etiquette to follow: Keep your pet on a leash in public places, always pick up after them, and show consideration for other road users.

Verify pet limitations and policies: Check the regulations before to visiting whether there are any pet restrictions for Vermont state parks and hiking trails.

Taking Disabled People on Vacation

Vermont is dedicated to giving visitors of all abilities access to its scenic landscape and tourist attractions. Traveling with those who have disabilities, however, necessitates some more planning and preparation. Here is some advice about traveling in Vermont with those who have disabilities:

Look into accessible lodgings and destinations: Look for accommodations for persons with disabilities, such as wheelchair access, at hotels, vacation rentals, and attractions. Resources and information are available from the Vermont Department of Disabilities, Aging, and Independent Living.

Plan your travel: If you're traveling into Vermont, make ahead arrangements for wheelchair assistance with your airline. Additionally, think about leasing an accessible vehicle or utilizing wheelchair-accessible public transportation.

Pack the tools and supplies you'll need: Bring any tools you might need, like wheelchairs, walkers, or oxygen tanks, as well as any supplies and prescriptions you might need.

Plan some accessible outdoor activities. Vermont has much to choose from, including hiking, fishing, and skiing. Additionally, a lot of museums and attractions provide accessibility features for visitors with disabilities, like audio tours or tactile exhibits.

Make ahead contact with attractions: whether you want to go to a particular attraction, like a museum or amusement park, get in touch with them beforehand to find out whether they have any special services or accessibility features.

Think about using a travel agent: A trip that satisfies your unique needs and criteria can be planned and booked with the assistance of a travel agent who specializes in accessible travel.

Be ready for crises: Be sure to have a strategy in place in case of unanticipated equipment breakdowns or medical issues. Maintain a handy list of medical information and emergency contacts.

With the right planning and preparation, traveling in Vermont with children, animals, or individuals with disabilities can be a joyful and gratifying experience. Vermont has something for everyone, including accessible attractions, pet-friendly lodgings, and family-friendly activities. You can ensure that everyone has a secure, pleasurable, and memorable vacation by paying attention to these suggestions and completing your homework beforehand.

CHAPTER THREE

Exploring Vermont`s Cities & Towns

Burlington

The main city in Vermont, Burlington, is a thriving college town located on Lake Champlain's eastern shore. For anyone visiting the Green Mountain State, Burlington is a must-visit location because of its stunning views, quaint streets, and lively culture. The best places to eat, shop, and enjoy the nightlife in Burlington will all be covered in-depth in this chapter.

Attractions

Visitors may enjoy a wide variety of attractions in Burlington. The University of Vermont, a stunning campus with a variety of historic buildings and lovely green areas, is located in the city. Visitors have a choice between joining a guided tour led by current students or taking a self-guided tour of the campus.

The Church Street Marketplace is one of Burlington's most well-liked attractions. A wide range of stores, eateries, and cafes fill this pedestrian-only boulevard. Spending hours perusing the shops, trying the regional food, and people-watching from one of the many outdoor cafes is possible for visitors.

The waterfront park in Burlington is yet another must-see destination. This lovely park offers breathtaking views of the Adirondack Mountains as it stretches along the shores of Lake Champlain. The many trails in the park can be explored on a rented bike, visitors can simply unwind on the beach and enjoy the sunshine, or they can take a leisurely stroll along the boardwalk.

The Ethan Allen Homestead is a must-see destination for history buffs. Ethan Allen, a Revolutionary War hero and one of Vermont's founders, originally lived at this significant location. Visitors can take a look around the house and grounds while learning about the local history.

Restaurants

With a large selection of restaurants serving anything from farm-to-table meals to foreign cuisine, Burlington is a food lover's heaven. The Farmhouse Tap & Grill is one of Burlington's most well-known eateries. This restaurant offers a seasonal menu and purchases its food from neighborhood farms. Visitors can eat things like hand-cut fries, specialty beer, and grass-fed burgers.

Hen of the Wood is yet another well-liked eatery in Burlington. This upmarket restaurant provides an exceptional wine list in addition to its farm-to-table menu. In a warm and welcoming setting, guests may savor meals like roasted duck, grilled steak, and wood-fired pizza.

Visitors should go to the Penny Cluse Cafe for a sample of Vermont's renowned maple syrup. A selection of breakfast options is available at this lovely diner, including the well-known "Penny Cluse," a plate of two eggs, toast, and homefries covered in maple gravy. Additionally, homemade baked goods, freshly squeezed juices, and locally roasted coffee are available to visitors.

Shopping

Burlington is a fantastic destination for consumers searching for something a little different because it is home to a range of distinctive and independent stores. The Church Street Marketplace is one of Burlington's most well-liked shopping areas. Numerous stores, including both big-box stores and independent shops, line this pedestrian-only street.

The Burlington Farmers' Market offers visitors a distinctive shopping experience. From May through October, a variety of local sellers sell everything from fresh produce to homemade crafts at this outdoor market. Visitors can peruse the market, enjoy regional cuisine, and purchase mementos for their homes.

The North End in Burlington is yet another fantastic place to shop. Vintage apparel boutiques, art galleries, and independent bookshops are just a few of the stores and galleries that call this colorful neighborhood home. Visitors can lose hours wandering the lovely lanes of the area and finding hidden treasures.

evening Burlington boasts a thriving evening culture with a range of bars and clubs that cater to different tastes. The Vermont Pub & Brewery is among Burlington's most well-liked bars. This neighborhood brewery serves a selection of artisan brews and pub fare, and on the weekends, live music is frequently performed there. Visitors can take in the laid-back ambiance and try some of Vermont's best beers.

Visitors should check out Leunig's Bistro & Cafe for a more upmarket evening experience. Small meals, wine, and a range of beverages are available at this classy French café. Jazz musicians perform live, and guests can take in the chic ambiance.

Club Metronome is the venue to go to if dancing is more your style. This nightclub has a large dance floor, a bustling ambiance, and a diversity of music, from electronic to hip-hop. The nightlife is exciting and lively, and guests can dance the night away.

Burlington is a bustling city with a wide selection of activities, eateries, shops, and places to go out at night. Visitors can stroll around the Church Street Marketplace's shops and cafes, take in the breathtaking views of Lake Champlain from the waterfront park, and explore the historic University of Vermont campus. The diversity of farm-to-table eateries will delight foodies, while shoppers will enjoy finding distinctive and independent stores in the North End area. Additionally, Burlington has a diverse nightlife scene with something for everyone for those seeking a fun night out. Anyone exploring Vermont must pay Burlington a visit.

Montpelier

The state capital of Vermont, Montpelier, is one of the most intriguing and distinctive of the state's lovely villages and small communities. The small city of Montpelier, which has a population of just over 7,000, is situated in the center of Vermont. Despite its tiny size, Montpelier is a center for outdoor leisure, culture, and history.

This section will discuss some of the top attractions in Montpelier, including its museums, landmarks, and outdoor pursuits. Everyone can find something to enjoy in Montpelier, regardless of their interest in history, art, or the great outdoors.

History of Montpelier

Examining Montpelier's past is crucial if you want to comprehend it completely. Founded in 1781,

Montpelier became the state capital in 1805. The city was a significant player in the Civil War, acting as the hub of the Union Army's operations in Vermont. Numerous historic sites and landmarks that honor Montpelier's lengthy history can be found there today.

The Vermont State House is one of Montpelier's most well-known historic locations. One of the oldest and best-preserved state capitols in the nation, the State House, a spectacular example of Greek Revival architecture, was completed in 1859. In addition to learning more about the State House's history and design, visitors can take a guided tour and even observe the legislature in session.

The Ethan Allen Homestead Museum in Montpelier is yet another important historical place. This museum, which is close to the city, honors the life and contributions of Revolutionary War hero Ethan Allen, who was also a significant figure in the early history of Vermont. Visitors can tour Allen's farm, discover more about his involvement in the American Revolution, and even see some of his personal effects.

The Museums of Montpelier

A number of museums that highlight the vibrant culture and history of the city are also located in Montpelier. A fantastic place to start is the Vermont Historical Society Museum, which has displays that emphasize the history and culture of the state from its earliest times to the present. Visitors can view artifacts, images, and papers that provide historical context for Vermont.

The T.W. Wood Gallery & Arts Center is a noteworthy museum in Montpelier. T.W. Wood, a Vermont artist, as well as other local artists, have exhibited in this museum. Art aficionados must visit the museum, which hosts changing exhibits of paintings, sculptures, and other pieces of artwork.

The Outdoor Activities in Montpelier

Montpelier is a terrific place to enjoy the outdoors in addition to its museums and historic monuments. Hiking is among the most well-liked outdoor pursuits in Montpelier. Beautiful mountains and forests encircle the city, and there are numerous trails that provide breathtaking panoramas of the surroundings. A fantastic location to start is Hubbard Park, which has a number of hiking routes that wind through the forest and provide stunning views over the city.

Skiing is another well-liked outdoor activity in Montpelier. The area around the city is home to some of the best skiing in the Northeast, including Sugarbush Resort and Stowe Mountain Resort. During the winter, visitors can hit the slopes to take in the stunning scenery and new powder.

The restaurants and stores in Montpelier

Without trying some of the mouthwatering cuisines and perusing the city's distinctive stores, a trip to Montpelier would be incomplete. Skinny Pancake, one of Montpelier's most well-known eateries, offers mouthwatering crepes, sandwiches, and salads crafted using regionally sourced ingredients. Positive Pie is a fantastic eatery that serves a range of pizzas and other Italian cuisine.

Montpelier offers a wide selection of distinctive stores and boutiques to peruse for those who want to go shopping. Capitol Stationers, which carries a large selection of stationery, cards, and gifts, is one of the most well-known stores in the area. Bear Pond Books is another fantastic place to browse. It has a huge range of new and old books as well as a pleasant café where customers can relax and have a cup of coffee and a pastry.

Festivals and Events in Montpelier

Additionally, Montpelier is renowned for hosting exciting events and festivals all year long. The Montpelier Farmers Market, which takes place every Saturday from May to October, is one of the most well-liked occasions. The market offers a variety of vendors offering local goods like fresh vegetables, baked goods, and other goods created in the area, as well as live entertainment.

The Montpelier Art Walk, which happens on the first Friday of every month, is another well-liked occasion. Throughout the city, galleries and studios stay open late during the art walk to display the creations of regional artists. Visitors can enjoy refreshments and live music while perusing the artwork and speaking with the artists.

A range of things to see and do are available in Montpelier, a small city with a huge personality, for tourists of all ages and interests. Everyone can find something to enjoy in Montpelier, whether they are interested in history, art, outdoor activities, or simply discovering new shops and eateries. Montpelier is a must-visit location for anybody visiting Vermont because of its historical landmarks, museums, and exciting events.

Stowe

Stowe, Vermont, is a charming town that provides countless options for outdoor activities, cultural encounters, and leisurely retreats. It is located in the heart of the Green Mountains. Some of the best ski resorts in the nation are located in Stowe, the "Ski Capital of the East," but there is much more to discover here than just the slopes. Everyone may find something to enjoy in Stowe, whether they are adventure seekers or nature lovers.

Sports Resorts

The ski resorts in Stowe are very popular and for good reason. Winter sports fans must visit the town because it is home to two top-notch resorts, Stowe Mountain Resort, and Smugglers' Notch Resort. The highest point in Vermont, Mount Mansfield, is home to the Stowe Mountain Resort, which has 116 routes spread across 485 acres of skiable land with a vertical drop of 2,360 feet. The resort is renowned for its difficult expert runs, which include the well-known "Front Four" of National, Liftline, Starr, and Goat. However, the resort also offers Nordic skiing, snowshoeing, and ice skating, and there are plenty of runs for skiers and snowboarders of all skill levels.

Another well-liked ski resort may be found not far from Stowe, called Smugglers' Notch Resort. The ski area is renowned for its welcoming atmosphere for families and beginner-friendly terrain, but it also includes a ton of difficult routes for more experienced skiers and snowboarders. The resort offers a range of indoor sports like swimming and rock climbing, as well as skiing, snowboarding, cross-country skiing, snowshoeing, and ice skating.

Outdoor Recreation

Stowe offers year-round outdoor activities, making it more than just a winter vacation spot. The town is a well-liked location for hiking, riding, and kayaking in the summer. The famed Long Trail, which runs 273 miles from Massachusetts to Canada and passes through Stowe, is one of many hiking paths in and surrounding the town. The route is a wonderful opportunity to enjoy Vermont's natural beauty and provides breathtaking vistas of the Green Mountains. Another well-liked trail is the 5.3-mile paved Stowe Recreation Path, which goes through the town and provides beautiful views of the mountains and river.

More heart-pounding activities are available in abundance in Stowe for those seeking them. Numerous zipline tours that soar through the treetops while providing breathtaking views of the mountains are available in the town. A number of businesses also provide hot air balloon rides, which are a special opportunity to take in Vermont's splendor from above. A number of neighborhood businesses provide guided climbs for climbers of all skill levels in Stowe, another well-liked location for rock climbing.

Events

There are several annual events that highlight the charm and personality of Stowe, a charming town with a thriving cultural life. The Stowe Winter Carnival is a week-long celebration of winter sports and activities that takes place every January. The festival features torchlight descents down the slopes, ski races, ice-cutting contests, and live music. The Stowe Farmer's Market, which features regional farmers and artisans offering fresh vegetables, baked goods, and crafts, is a well-liked destination during the summer. From May through

October, the market is hosted every Sunday and is a wonderful chance to sample Vermont's regional cuisine.

An additional well-liked occasion that draws foodies from all around the area is the Stowe Wine and Food Classic, which takes place in August. The event features regional chefs and wineries and offers wine tastings, cooking demonstrations, and courses on wine pairing. The Stowe Tango Music Festival, a celebration of the Argentine tango with live music, workshops, and dance performances, is another well-liked event. Both are held in October and include the work of local artists.

Additionally, the town of Stowe is home to a number of museums and historical sites. The Vermont Ski and Snowboard Museum, which is near Stowe, honors the state's long history of skiing and has displays on how skiing, snowboarding, and other winter sports have changed over time. The museum also holds occasions and movie showings all year long. Through its displays and artifacts, the Stowe Historical Society Museum in the town's heart provides a window into Stowe's past. The museum provides guided walking tours of the community and is housed in a historic structure that was previously a schoolhouse.

Stowe offers many opportunities for people seeking to unwind. Numerous spas and wellness facilities that provide massages, facials, and other treatments are located in the town. A well-liked location with a heated outdoor pool, hot tubs with mountain views, and a full range of spa services is the Stoweflake Mountain Resort & Spa. Another well-liked destination is the Trapp Family Lodge, established by the illustrious von Trapp family from "The Sound of Music," which features an opulent spa in addition to a wide selection of outdoor sports.

A variety of eateries and cafes providing delectable regional fare can be found all across Stowe. The community is renowned for its farm-to-table philosophy, and numerous restaurants use produce from nearby growers and producers. In a former grist mill, The Hen of the Wood is a well-liked destination for fine dining. Dishes are served here using ingredients that are in season and are sourced nearby. Another well-liked location is the Piecasso Pizzeria and Lounge, which offers craft beers and wood-fired pizzas in a relaxed, family-friendly setting.

Anyone seeking outdoor adventures, cultural encounters, and relaxation should make a trip to Stowe, Vermont. Stowe has something for everyone with its top-notch ski resorts, year-round recreational activities, active cultural scenes, and breathtaking natural beauty.

Woodstock

A charming community called Woodstock is located right in the middle of Vermont's Green Mountains. This small town is well known for its lovely shops, colorful festivals, and covered bridges that draw tourists from all over the world. This section will discuss the top activities and sights in Woodstock, including its rich past, beautiful surroundings, and upcoming cultural events.

Background of Woodstock

Due to its location on the Ottauquechee River, which offered water power for mills and factories, Woodstock was colonized in the late 18th century and quickly developed into a bustling village. The town remained prosperous well into the 19th century when it developed into a center for the wool industry, creating high-quality wool products that were exported throughout the nation.

Early in the 20th century, artists and authors who were looking for inspiration in its stunning natural surroundings started to flock to Woodstock. Famous visitors who spent time in the area and wrote about its allure included Sinclair Lewis, Robert Frost, and Ernest Hemingway.

The covered bridges of Woodstock

The town's covered bridges are among its most well-known landmarks. The Middle Bridge sometimes referred to as the "kissing bridge," is arguably the most well-known. To replace a previous bridge that had been destroyed by flooding, it was constructed in 1969. The custom of couples standing on the covered walkway and exchanging kisses gave rise to the bridge's name.

In Woodstock, the Taftsville Covered Bridge is another must-see sight. It is one of Vermont's oldest covered bridges and dates back to 1836. The Ottauquechee River offers breathtaking vistas as you cross the bridge.

natural landmarks

The Green Mountains, Quechee Gorge, and Marsh-Billings-Rockefeller National Historical Park are just a few of the stunning natural features that surround Woodstock. George Perkins Marsh, a conservationist who played a key role in the development of the national park system in the 19th century, previously owned the 550-acre home that now serves as the park.

The park has a number of hiking paths, including the short and lovely Marsh-Billings-Rockefeller Loop Trail, which leads tourists past the famed Marsh-Billings-Rockefeller Mansion and through a lovely forest. The mansion offers guided tours and displays authentic Rockefeller family furnishings and artwork.

Cultural occasions and celebrations

In addition to numerous annual events and festivals honoring the community's history and legacy, Woodstock is renowned for its thriving arts and cultural scene.

The Woodstock Vermont Film Series, which takes place every year from October to April, is one of the most well-known events. At the Town Hall Theater, these independent and foreign films are shown as part of the series. There are also post-movie interviews with the directors, producers, and other members of the film business.

The annual Woodstock Art Festival, which takes place in June, is another well-liked occasion. Local and regional artists who exhibit their work in a range of media, such as painting, sculpture, and photography, are included at the festival.

The town also organizes a number of wine and culinary festivals throughout the year, such as the Woodstock Vermont Wine and Culinary Festival, the Woodstock Vermont Cheese Festival, and the Woodstock Vermont Pie Festival.

dining and shopping

With hundreds of unique shops and galleries selling anything from handmade pottery to antique furniture, Woodstock's downtown district is a shopper's delight. The Unicorn, a well-known local establishment that offers fine handcrafted products including ceramics, jewelry, and textiles, is one of the most well-liked stores.

Everyone can find a place to eat in Woodstock, which offers everything from quick eateries to elegant dining establishments. The Red Rooster, which offers farm-to-table cuisine created using locally sourced ingredients, is one of the town's most well-known eateries.

Be sure to explore some of Woodstock's well-known sites, like the Middle Bridge and Taftsville Covered Bridge, if you're planning a trip there. Hike through the Marsh-Billings-Rockefeller National Historical Park to discover the breathtaking natural settings that have served as a source of inspiration for so many authors and artists over the years.

Don't pass up the exciting festivals and cultural events that take place in Woodstock, such as the Woodstock Art Festival, Woodstock Film Series, and Woodstock Vermont Wine and Food Festival. Of course, you should also indulge in some of the town's delectable fare, including farm-to-table meals made with regional ingredients and some of Vermont's world-famous pies and cheeses.

There are several alternatives for accommodations in Woodstock, ranging from little beds and breakfasts to opulent inns and hotels. One of the town's most well-liked lodging options is the Woodstock Inn and Resort, which features opulent rooms and suites, a full-service spa, and a number of extras.

Anyone visiting Vermont should make sure to stop in at Woodstock. It is a remarkable gem in the Green Mountains because of its extensive history, stunning scenery, cultural activities, and distinctive dining and retail options. So prepare to explore all that Woodstock has to offer by packing your bags!

Manchester

Greetings from the Green Mountain State, Vermont! Look no further than Manchester if you're looking for a quaint town with a mix of outlet shopping, art galleries, and golf courses. Whether you're a golf fan, a shopaholic, or an art enthusiast, Manchester, which is located in the southern section of the state, has something for you.

Shopping

Manchester is a fantastic location if you enjoy shopping. You can find some excellent prices at the more than 40 outlet stores, which feature well-known labels like Polo Ralph Lauren, Coach, and Kate Spade. Because the Manchester Designer Outlets are in the middle of the city, you can easily spend the entire day looking around and shopping there.

But in Manchester, big brands aren't everything. The community's local retail sector is likewise growing, with individual stores and boutiques selling everything from clothing to jewelry to home furnishings. Our favorites are as follows:

The Northshire Bookstore is a well-known neighborhood landmark that has been operating for more than 40 years and provides a vast assortment of books, presents, and games. Even a cozy cafe is available for you to visit while sipping coffee and relaxing with a good book.

Manchester Woodcraft is the place to go if you're seeking stunning, handcrafted wooden furniture and home decor. Everything is manufactured in Vermont by professional artisans who follow environmentally friendly procedures.

Since 1977, Mother Myrick's Confectionery in Manchester has offered custom-made chocolates, fudge, toffee, and other confections. Try the renowned Buttercrunch for sure!

Manchester has a surprising amount to offer art enthusiasts. It has a long history of drawing painters and other creative types to the area, and it continues to do so today. There are numerous galleries in the city that display a variety of genres and mediums.

The Southern Vermont Arts Center is a nonprofit arts organization with a lovely site that includes galleries, studios, and performance spaces. It has been established since 1922. They provide instruction and workshops in a variety of fields, including pottery, photography, and painting.

This modern art gallery, Gallery North Star, specializes in big, vivid pieces by both local and international artists. Additionally, they provide framing and art consulting services.

The Equinox Village complex's Hunter Gallery of Fine Art is a gallery that features both classic and contemporary works of art created by Vermont artists. Outside, there is a sculpture garden as well.

Golf

Golfers will be happy to learn that Manchester is home to several of the state's top courses. The town's charming setting, tucked away in the Green Mountains, provides some breathtaking golfing views.

Walter Travis, a famous golf course architect, created the stunning 18-hole golf course at the historic Equinox Golf Resort & Spa. Play on the course is hard, and the scenery is stunning.

The classic 18-hole course at the private Manchester Country Club is renowned for its immaculate fairways and greens. A driving range, practice green, and pro shop are also available.

Although technically outside of Manchester, Stratton Mountain Resort is close by and provides another top-notch golfing option. Geoffrey Cornish created their 27-hole course, which has played host to several prestigious competitions.

Addition to Golf, Art, and Shopping

Manchester offers much more than just shopping, art, and golf, of course. While you're here, check out and perform the following other things:

The Equinox Preserve hike: Just outside of town, on a 914-acre nature preserve, are miles of hiking paths that wind through picturesque meadows and forests. Make sure to visit Mount Equinox's summit, which provides sweeping views of the mountains in the area.

Visit the American Museum of Fly Fishing, which is a must-see for anyone interested in the development of fly fishing. It is housed in a historic structure on Main Street. Additionally, to constantly changing exhibits and educational activities, they have a sizable collection of artifacts and memorabilia.

Take a picturesque drive; Manchester, Vermont, which is noted for its beautiful fall foliage, is no exception. Drive through the town on Route 7A to take in the stunning scenery and vibrant leaves.

Investigate your community's past: Manchester has a long history that dates back to the early 19th century. Take a guided tour of one of the numerous historic buildings in the area, such as the Wilburton Inn, the Hildene Estate (once Robert Todd Lincoln's house), or the 1761 House to discover more about the town's past.

The Southern Vermont Arts & Crafts Festival, the Manchester Food & Wine Classic, and the Equinox Valley Nursery Fall Festival are just a few of the festivals that Manchester hosts all year long. For a schedule of events during your visit, consult the neighborhood calendar.

Places to Stay

From quaint bed and breakfasts to five-star resorts, Manchester and its surroundings offer a variety of excellent lodging choices.

One of Manchester's most recognizable buildings, The Equinox Golf Resort & Spa has a long history that dates back to 1769. They provide a selection of rooms and suites in addition to a number of on-site dining establishments and a full-service spa.

The Inn at Manchester: This delightful bed and breakfast is situated in the center of the city and provides comfortable rooms with modern conveniences. Each morning, they also provide a delectable brunch.

The Taconic: This boutique hotel is situated just outside of the city and offers a contemporary, chic ambiance with stunning mountain views. They have a heated outdoor pool, a restaurant, and a bar on the premises.

Manchester is a wonderful location in Vermont whether you're a shopper, an art enthusiast, a golfer, or just seeking for a quaint tiny town to explore. You're sure to have a great time with its variety of outlet shopping, art galleries, and golf courses, along with many other things to see and do. So grab your bags and travel to the Green Mountain State to find this hidden treasure!

Brattleboro

Southeast Vermont's quaint little town of Brattleboro offers a special fusion of creative flair, town spirit, and scenic beauty. The town, which is known for its growing craft brewers, bustling farmers' markets, and dynamic arts scene, is located in the foothills of the Green Mountains. The main attractions of Brattleboro, as well as some of its fascinating history and cultural heritage, will be discussed in this section.

Background of Brattleboro

Early in the 18th century, when Europeans first began to settle there, is when Brattleboro first became known. The town was originally a part of the 17th-century land grant made to the Massachusetts Bay Colony, but in 1777, when Vermont proclaimed its independence from England, it was incorporated into the new state. The town bears the name of Colonel William Brattle, Jr., a prominent landowner and one of Harvard College's founders.

Brattleboro has developed through time from a sleepy rural hamlet to a vibrant city with a flourishing arts and culture scene. The town also had a significant impact on American history by acting as a hub for the anti-nuclear movement in the 1970s and as a stop on the Underground Railroad during the Civil War.

Activities and Attractions in Brattleboro

Culture and the Arts

The town of Brattleboro is home to numerous galleries and performing venues, and it is well renowned for its thriving arts scene. The Brattleboro Museum and Art Center, which showcases a changing collection of modern art and historical relics from the area, is a must-see for art enthusiasts. Another well-liked location for art and culture is the Latchis Theater, which presents live performances and movie showings all year long.

The town also hosts a number of yearly celebrations of the arts, such as the Brattleboro Literary Festival and the Strolling of the Heifers Parade, which showcases ornate floats and performances influenced by the town's agricultural past.

Markets for produce

Additionally well-known in Brattleboro are the thriving farmer's markets that take place all year long. The biggest and most well-known farmers market is in Brattleboro, where dozens of merchants provide a variety of goods including baked goods, meats, cheeses, and fresh produce. From May through October, the market is open every Saturday and is a terrific place to sample some of the greatest foods and beverages in the area.

artisanal breweries

Finally, there are a number of craft breweries in Brattleboro that are worth visiting. A local favorite, The Whetstone Station Restaurant, and Brewery offers a variety of delectable brews and pub fare in a rural setting with views of the Connecticut River. Hermit Thrush Brewery, which specializes in sour beers, and McNeill's Brewery, which has been making top-notch craft beers since 1992, are two other well-known brewers in the region.

Investigating Brattleboro

Small and straightforward to navigate on foot, Brattleboro is a town. Start your day at the Brattleboro Common, a popular meeting spot where activities and music are held all year round. After that, proceed to Main Street, which is dotted with boutiques, art galleries, and coffee shops. Make sure to visit Everyone's Books, a reputable independent bookshop in the area that has been helping the neighborhood for more than 35 years.

After that, proceed to the River Garden, a public area where activities like exhibits and plays take place all year long. The Brattleboro Area Chamber of Commerce is based at the River Garden, where you may pick up brochures and details about the town and neighborhood.

A stroll along the Connecticut River, which separates Vermont and New Hampshire, is the final activity. Along the river, there are many parks and walking trails, including the West River Trail, which provides breathtaking views of the mountains and surrounding area.

Accommodations and Dining

In Brattleboro, there are many places to stay, including charming bed and breakfasts, inviting inns, and inexpensive hotels. The Latchis Hotel and Theatre is a special choice that fuses traditional elegance with contemporary conveniences, including a restaurant and movie theater.

Brattleboro offers a wide variety of dining alternatives for every taste and price range. Try the Down Home Kitchen for breakfast or brunch; it serves delectable homemade biscuits, ingredients from the neighborhood, and live music on the weekends. Visit Duo Restaurant for lunch or dinner for innovative farm-to-table fare crafted using regional ingredients. The Whetstone Station Restaurant and Brewery and the Brattleboro Food Co-op, which provides a broad variety of fresh, wholesome foods and snacks, are two more well-liked dining establishments.

Days off in Brattleboro

While there are many nearby attractions and day trip possibilities, Brattleboro is a destination unto itself. A major ski resort, Mount Snow, which offers skiing, snowboarding, and other winter activities during the colder months, is only a short drive away. Mount Snow provides magnificent chairlift rides, hiking, and mountain biking throughout the summer.

The Vermont Country Store, which is situated in the lovely community of Weston, is another close destination. The shop sells a variety of goods that are produced in the area, such as maple syrup, cheddar cheese, and homemade fudge. Visitors can also take a tour of the nearby Benedictine monastery of Weston Priory, which also welcomes them for worship and retreats.

A beautiful tiny town, Brattleboro offers a special fusion of creative flair, civic pride, and scenic beauty. Brattleboro is a must-see location for anybody visiting Vermont, whether they want to take in the breathtaking natural beauty, sample the fresh local cuisine and drink, or explore the town's thriving arts scene.

CHAPTER FOUR

Vermont's Natural Wonders

Green Mountains

Vermont is renowned for its natural beauty, and the Green Mountains are at the heart of it all. Spanning the length of the state, these rolling hills and peaks offer a wealth of outdoor activities, from hiking and biking to skiing and snowshoeing. But the Green Mountains are not just a playground for the adventurous – they are also home to some of the most spectacular fall foliage displays in the country. In this chapter, we will explore the best ways to experience Vermont's natural wonders in the Green Mountains.

Hiking in the Green Mountains

The Green Mountains are a hiker's paradise, with hundreds of miles of trails winding through forests, over ridges, and up to high peaks. Some of the most popular hiking destinations include Mount Mansfield, Camel's Hump, and the Long Trail, which runs the length of the state. But there are also plenty of lesser-known trails that offer a quieter, more secluded experience.

One of the best places to start your hiking adventures in the Green Mountains is Mount Mansfield, the highest peak in Vermont. From the summit, hikers can enjoy panoramic views of the surrounding landscape, including Lake Champlain and the Adirondacks in New York. The hike to the top can be challenging, but there are several trails to choose from, ranging in difficulty from easy to strenuous.

For a more off-the-beaten-path experience, consider hiking to the summit of Camel's Hump. This iconic peak is known for its distinctive hump-shaped profile, and the trail to the top offers stunning views of the surrounding forests and valleys. The hike can be steep and rocky in places, but the rewards are well worth the effort.

If you're looking for a multi-day hiking adventure, consider tackling the Long Trail. This 273-mile trail runs the length of Vermont, from the Massachusetts border to the Canadian border, and offers hikers a chance to explore some of the state's most remote and scenic areas. Hikers have the option of staying in shelters, campsites, or more opulent hotels in adjacent towns along the way.

Biking in the Green Mountains

The Green Mountains are also a popular destination for cyclists, with miles of scenic roads and challenging mountain bike trails to explore. Some of the most popular cycling routes include the Green Mountain Byway, the Lamoille Valley Rail Trail, and the Kingdom Trails.

The Green Mountain Byway is an 11-mile scenic route that winds through the heart of the Green Mountains, from Stowe to Waterbury. Along the way, cyclists can enjoy views of Mount Mansfield, the Worcester Range, and the Mad River Valley. The route is mostly flat, with a few gentle hills, making it a great option for cyclists of all levels.

For a longer, more challenging ride, consider the Lamoille Valley Rail Trail. This 93-mile trail follows the path of an old railway through the heart of Vermont's Northeast Kingdom, offering cyclists a chance to explore some of the state's most remote and scenic areas. Cycling enthusiasts can take in vistas of the Green Mountains, sweeping farmland, and charming New England towns along the route.

Mountain bikers will find plenty to love in the Green Mountains, too. The Kingdom Trails in East Burke are widely considered to be some of the best mountain biking trails in the country, with over 100 miles of trails winding through dense forests and over rugged terrain. The trails range from easy to expert, making them a great option for riders of all levels.

Skiing in the Green Mountains

When the snow falls, the Green Mountains transform into a winter wonderland, with some of the best skiing and snowboarding in the Northeast. From family-friendly resorts to challenging backcountry terrain, there is something for everyone in the Green Mountains.

One of the most popular ski resorts in the Green Mountains is Stowe Mountain Resort. With over 300 inches of snowfall annually, this resort offers some of the best skiing and snowboarding in the state. The resort features 116 trails, ranging from beginner to expert, as well as a variety of terrain parks and halfpipes. In addition to skiing and snowboarding, visitors can also enjoy snowshoeing, cross-country skiing, and ice skating.

Lake Champlain

The largest naturally occurring freshwater lake in Vermont, Lake Champlain, stretches more than 120 miles from the Canadian border to the south. The lake is well-known for its stunning natural surroundings, varied animals, and a wealth of leisure options. It provides guests with the opportunity to get away into the forest, unwind on its pristine beaches, or partake in exhilarating water sports. Anyone visiting Vermont should make sure to visit Lake Champlain.

using a boat on Lake Champlain

Each and every traveler should experience the fun of boating on Lake Champlain. The lake has a substantial stretch of boating-friendly navigable waters. The numerous coves, islets, and secret bays of the lake can be explored by visitors who rent boats or join guided tours. Visitors can easily launch their boats at the lake's numerous marinas and boat launch facilities.

Kayaking, paddle boarding, and canoeing are all excellent activities that may be enjoyed in the lake's clear, tranquil waters. There are numerous lovely parks and beaches along the lake's shores, so it's simple to pull up and have a picnic or go swimming. With a variety of fish species living in its waters, including trout, salmon, and bass, the lake also provides a wealth of fishing options.

on Lake Champlain, fishing

Fishermen love Lake Champlain because it is a haven for them. The lake is a great place for anglers because of its beautiful waters, which are home to a variety of fish. Fishing enthusiasts can enjoy catching salmon, trout, bass, walleye, and northern pike, among other species. The shallow bays and coves of the lake make it a great place to catch larger predators because they are the perfect home for smaller fish.

Fishing techniques available to visitors include fly fishing, spinning, and trolling. The lake is accessible for fishing year-round, but spring and fall are the greatest seasons. The lake's waters are cooler and the fish are more active at these times, making it simpler to land a trophy-sized fish.

A local guide can be hired by tourists to show them the greatest lakes for fishing. These experts can assist visitors in landing the fish of their dreams because they are quite knowledgeable about the lake's biology. Visitors can also take advantage of fishing charters and tours, which come complete with all the necessary gear for a productive fishing session.

the Lake Champlain beaches

Numerous stunning beaches on Lake Champlain give visitors a chance to unwind and enjoy the sunshine. The sandy beaches by the lake are ideal for picnics, swimming, and sunbathing. The beaches are perfect for guests of all ages since they are pristine, well-kept, and family-friendly.

On Lake Champlain, North Beach, Oakledge Park, and Sand Bar State Park are a few of the well-liked beaches. The most populous city in Vermont, Burlington, is home to North Beach, which is a favorite among both locals and tourists. The beach is ideal for swimming and other water sports because of its long sandy shore and beautiful seas.

A few minutes south of Burlington, on Lake Champlain, Oakledge Park is another well-liked beach. There are walking routes, picnic spaces, playgrounds, and a large sandy beach in the park. Renting kayaks and paddleboards is an option for visitors, as is joining a tour of the lake from the park.

On the southern end of the lake, Sand Bar State Park is a well-liked beach destination. There is a boat launch, a picnic area, hiking trails, and a sandy beach in the park. In the park, visitors can also go fishing and observe birds and other wildlife.

Visitors to Lake Champlain can take a leisurely boat trip, explore the many islands, coves, and bays, or partake in more daring water activities to take advantage of the lake's splendor. The quiet waters and peaceful environment of the lake can be experienced by guests when kayaking, paddle boarding, or canoeing.

Lake Champlain is a sanctuary for fishermen. Visitors can try their hand at catching a trophy-sized fish because the waters there are home to a variety of fish species. Visitors can hire fishing guides to show them the finest locations and methods for catching the fish they want.

The sandy beaches around the lake provide guests with a chance to unwind and enjoy the sunshine.

Visitors can make use of the many well-kept and kid-friendly beaches to go swimming, tanning, and picnicking. The parks close by offer chances for hiking, birdwatching, and wildlife observation.

Every visitor to Vermont needs to enjoy Lake Champlain, a natural wonder. Families, couples, and solitary tourists will find it to be an amazing vacation because of its beauty and variety of recreational possibilities. Everyone can find something to do in Lake Champlain, from boating and fishing to lounging on the beach.

Quechee Gorge

Vermont is home to an abundance of breathtaking natural beauty. One of the most breathtaking locations to see is Quechee Gorge, which is a short distance from Woodstock in the beautiful hamlet of Quechee. Quechee Gorge offers something for everyone, whether you're searching for a breathtaking drive, a strenuous walk, or just want to take in the scenery. We'll look at all the ways you may take advantage of this breathtaking natural wonder in this section.

The Ottauquechee River carved up the deep, stony gorge known as Quechee Gorge over thousands of years. One of Vermont's most stunning natural attractions, the gorge is nearly 165 feet deep and one mile long. A favorite location for nature lovers, the area surrounding the gorge is also home to a varied range of plant and animal species.

Stunning Drive

Taking a beautiful drive is one of the greatest ways to enjoy Quechee Gorge. The Quechee Gorge Village, which is close to Route 4, is a good place to start. Before heading out on the road, browse the many stores and restaurants in this area, which has ample parking.

From there, you can travel the 5.2-mile Quechee Gorge Scenic Drive, which follows the Ottauquechee River's twisting course. Driving through some of Vermont's most scenic landscapes, you'll see views of rolling hills, sleepy villages, and, of course, the magnificent canyon itself.

You'll pass by a number of pull-offs and overlooks along the way where you may pause and enjoy the scenery. The Quechee Canyon Bridge, which spans the canyon and provides an amazing vantage point, is one of the most well-liked stops. Bring your camera; the bridge is an excellent place to take pictures.

Hiking

Hiking is a fantastic alternative if you're searching for a more active way to enjoy Quechee Gorge. You can select a hiking route in the area that meets your skill level because there are several of them and they range in difficulty from easy to difficult.

The Quechee Gorge Trail, a 1.6-mile loop that circles the gorge's rim, is one of the most well-known paths. The relatively simple trek provides breathtaking views of the gorge and the surrounding landscape. You can stop at a number of viewpoints along the trip to take in the view.

The Quechee Gorge region is traversed by the Appalachian Trail, which offers more difficult hikes. To reach the gorge, trek south for about three miles starting from Route 4. Although more difficult, this hike rewards hikers with breathtaking views of the river and surrounding forest.

Canyon Hiking

Gorge hiking is an exhilarating way for the most daring guests to explore Quechee Gorge. This activity entails hiking into the gorge itself and moving upstream along the river. Although the hike is difficult and requires caution, the payoff— spectacular views of the gorge from the bottom— is more than worthwhile.

The gorge can be reached by two different routes for trekking. The first method involves traveling down the spur route that descends into the canyon while on the Quechee Canyon route. The alternative option is to follow the river upstream on the trail that begins at the Quechee Gorge Bridge.

No matter which tracks you pick, gorge hiking is a memorable adventure that gives you a fresh viewpoint of the gorge. The hike can be challenging, so make sure to pack lots of water and food as well as appropriate hiking boots.

Other Activities

There are other activities in and around Quechee Gorge in addition to scenic driving, hiking, and gorge hiking.

Kayaking or canoeing on the Ottauquechee River is a well-liked pastime. There are various places along the river where you can hire kayaks or canoes, including Quechee Gorge Village. You can see the gorge and the surrounding area from a different angle as you paddle down the river.

Visit the adjacent Quechee State Park as an alternative. The park has picnic spots, bathing areas, hiking routes, and a campground for overnight stays. The park is a convenient stop on your journey because it is only a few kilometers from the gorge.

Be sure to stop by the neighboring Simon Pearce Mill if history interests you. The mill, which was constructed in 1766, today houses a glassblowing studio, a café, and a retail space. You may observe the glassblowers in action and buy lovely handcrafted glassware as a memento of your journey.

Last but not least, be sure to attend the Quechee Balloon Festival, which is held in June. Hot air balloon rides, live music, craft vendors, and more are all part of the celebration. It's a fascinating and enjoyable way to take in Quechee Gorge and Vermont's natural splendor.

Anyone traveling to Vermont must visit Quechee Gorge. There is something for everyone at Quechee Gorge, whether you choose a leisurely scenic drive, a strenuous climb, or an adventurous gorge hike. It's hardly surprising that it's regarded as one of Vermont's most magnificent natural attractions given its breathtaking natural beauty and plenty of outdoor recreation opportunities. Plan your trip to Quechee Gorge today to witness the magic yourself.

Mad River Valley

Vermont is noted for its magnificent natural settings. The Mad River Valley, a renowned location for outdoor enthusiasts, is situated in central Vermont and offers a range of activities, such as swimming, hiking, mountain biking, and skiing. The natural attractions of the Mad River Valley, such as its swimming holes, waterfalls, and mountain biking paths, will be the main topic of this section.

Swimming Holes: Swimming is one of the most well-liked summertime activities in the Mad River Valley. There are various swimming holes in the valley, each of which provides a distinctive experience. Warren Falls, a swimming hole not far from Route 100, is one of the most well-liked. Warren Falls is a collection of cascading waterfalls that empty into a number of swimming and sunbathing-friendly ponds. Visitors can take pleasure in diving into the pools from the rocks below or unwinding in the waterfall's natural Jacuzzi.

The Lareau Swim Hole, which is close to Waitsfield on the Mad River, is another well-liked swimming location. Families with little children will love this location because the water is quiet and shallow. Picnicking and sunbathing are popular activities for visitors on the river's grassy banks.

Visitors can check out the Blueberry Lake swimming hole, which is close to Warren, for a more private experience. This swimming hole offers a serene and peaceful setting and is surrounded by thick woodland. For swimming and diving, the water is perfectly clear and transparent.

Waterfalls: There are a number of waterfalls in the Mad River Valley, each of which offers a distinctive experience. Moss Glen Falls, which can be seen not far from Route 100, is among the most well-known waterfalls in the region. This waterfall creates an amazing scene as it rushes down over 125 feet of moss-covered rocks. Hikers can reach the falls and take in the scenery while eating a picnic lunch.

Texas Falls, which is close to Route 125, is another well-known waterfall in the region. This waterfall features various swimming and exploring-friendly basins where cascading cascades occur. Hikers can enjoy the magnificent views of the falls and surrounding woodland while traveling along the river.

Visitors can check out Bristol Falls in the adjacent town of Bristol for a more private waterfall experience. This waterfall is located in a serene and calm environment, surrounded by a thick forest. Swim in the pools at the base of the falls or strolling in the nearby forest are both options for visitors.

Mountain biking: The Mad River Valley is a well-liked destination for mountain bikers, with a variety of courses for riders of all experience levels. The Mad River Path, a 16-mile trail that travels beside the Mad River and through the surrounding woodland, is one of the most well-liked mountain biking routes in the region. The walk is ideal for novices and provides beautiful views of the nearby mountains and rivers.

The Sugarbush Resort has a number of downhill tracks with difficult terrain and spectacular valley vistas for more experienced mountain bikers. In order to make it simple for visitors to access the trails, the resort also provides a lift service.

The Blueberry Lake trails offer a network of trails that weave through thick forests and along the shores of Blueberry Lake for those seeking a more isolated mountain riding experience. The routes are ideal for intermediate and experienced riders and offer a diversity of terrain.

A real natural treasure, the Mad River Valley provides a range of activities for tourists of all ages and skill levels. The Mad River Valley is the ideal location for outdoor enthusiasts, whether you want to bathe in the Mad River's pure waters, explore the breathtaking waterfalls that flow through the valley, or test your mettle on the mountain biking routes. It's no surprise that the Mad River Valley is one of Vermont's top tourist destinations with its breathtaking natural surroundings and wealth of activities.

Ben & Jerry`s Factory

Ben & Jerry's, one of the most well-known companies in the world, was born in Vermont, a state known for its scenic beauty and quaint small communities. The ice cream shop, which was established in 1978 by two friends named Ben Cohen and Jerry Greenfield, has become a tourist attraction and a cultural landmark in the Green Mountain State.

The Ben & Jerry's Factory is situated in Waterbury, Vermont, a short distance from Montpelier, the state's capital. Visitors can take factory tours that give them an inside look at how the company makes its ice cream and the chance to sample some of the well-known varieties that have helped Ben & Jerry's become so well-known.

A brief video detailing the history of Ben & Jerry's, including the commitment to utilizing only premium, all-natural ingredients in their ice cream, is played before the factory tour. The actual factory is then shown to visitors so they may observe the production process in action.

The Flavor Lab, which develops and tests new flavors, is one of the tour's most fascinating stops. Visitors are welcome to tour the lab and perhaps try some of the developing experimental flavors.

The tasting area, where guests can sample some of the iconic Ben & Jerry's varieties that have become so adored worldwide, is, of course, the actual highlight of the trip.

Many different flavors are available, from the classic Cherry Garcia to more recent additions like Non-Dairy Caramel Almond Brittle. Even better, customers may mix and match various ice creams and toppings to create their own unique flavors.

The Ben & Jerry's Factory, however, offers much more than just mouthwatering ice cream. Visitors can discover more about the company's long-standing commitment to social and environmental justice during the tour. For instance, Ben & Jerry's has earned certification as a B Corporation, demonstrating that it upholds strict criteria for social and environmental responsibility.

A variety of interactive exhibits that further examine these topics are also available at the factory. The company's dedication to fair trade, its initiatives to lessen its carbon footprint, and its support for numerous social causes are all available for visitors to learn about.

There are a variety of other experiences available for individuals who want to delve even further into the world of Ben & Jerry's. The business offers a behind-the-scenes tour that immerses guests even further in the manufacturing process and gives them the chance to observe how the ice cream's renowned chunks and swirls are added.

Additionally, a variety of workshops and classes are offered, including a Flavor Lab Experience where guests can develop their own flavor from scratch. For those who take their ice cream seriously, there is even a five-day immersion program that offers an in-depth look at the Ben & Jerry's universe.

Without a stop at the Scoop Shop, of course, no trip to the Ben & Jerry's Factory would be complete. Here, guests can indulge in their preferred flavors in cones, cups, or even sundaes. Additionally, The Scoop Shop sells a range of goods, such as pint-sized ice cream containers, t-shirts, and hats.

Anyone who enjoys ice cream or is curious about the company's dedication to social and environmental responsibility must pay a visit to the Ben & Jerry's Factory. It is an event that is guaranteed to be remembered long after the last scoop has been enjoyed because of its fascinating tours, engaging exhibits, and mouthwatering flavors.

Shelburne Farms

Shelburne Farms, a 1,400-acre working farm that has been a landmark in Vermont for more than a century, is situated on the banks of Lake Champlain. Dr. William Seward Webb and his wife Lila Vanderbilt Webb founded the farm as a model farm and country residence in the late 19th century. Shelburne Farms is now a public attraction that gives guests a look into the past and present of Vermont's agricultural legacy.

History

A well-known businessman who played a significant role in the growth of the Adirondack and Green Mountain regions was Dr. William Seward Webb. He and his wife Lila Vanderbilt Webb made the decision to build a model farm in Vermont near Lake Champlain in the late 19th century. After buying more than 3,800 acres of land, they started the process of turning it into a functioning farm.

The Webbs employed Frederick Law Olmsted, a landscape designer best known for creating Central Park in New York City, to create their estate's grounds. Olmsted included features like a formal garden, a carriage house, and a horse stable in his design of the farm in order to make it both aesthetically pleasing and useful.

The farm expanded and changed over time, turning into a major supplier of superior dairy products. James Watson Webb, the son of the Webbs, and his wife Electra Havemeyer carried on expanding and enhancing the farm. The Shelburne Farms Foundation, which the family founded in 1972, turned the estate into a nonprofit institution devoted to sustainability and education.

Shelburne Farms is a leading example of sustainable agriculture and education today and a National Historic Landmark.

Farming Shelburne Farms is a thriving farm that produces premium dairy goods like yogurt, milk, and cheese. A herd of roughly 125 Brown Swiss cows, renowned for their kind disposition and great milk output, resides on the property.

The dairy barn is open for tours, allowing farm visitors to observe the cows being milked.

Additionally, they can go to the cheesemaking facility to see how the farm's celebrated cheddar cheese is made. Visitors can observe the milk being transformed into cheese and then being matured to perfection as the cheesemaking process is open to the public.

Shelburne Farms also produces a range of fruits and vegetables in addition to its dairy business. Visitors can observe how vegetables are grown and harvested in the farm's sizable market garden. Additionally, the farm makes maple syrup, a key component of Vermont agriculture.

Travel and Recreation

Take a guided tour of Shelburne Farms to learn about the farm's operations, history, and sustainability methods. The market garden, cheesemaking facility, and dairy barn are all included in the tour. A wagon trip through the farm's fields and forests allows visitors to take in the stunning views of the Champlain Valley.

Shelburne Farms offers a range of workshops and classes for people looking for a more practical education. Learn more about gardening, sustainable agriculture, producing cheese, and maple sugaring. A range of educational activities is also provided by the farm for use by school groups and other organizations.

Shelburne Farms is home to a multitude of hiking trails and outdoor activities in addition to its agricultural operations. Hiking through the farm's fields and forests, fishing in Lake Champlain, and seeing the lovely gardens are all available to visitors.

Sustainability

Shelburne Farms is dedicated to environmental responsibility and sustainability. The farm's operations are planned to have as little of an environmental impact as possible and to encourage sustainable farming. The farm heats its buildings with wood chips from sustainably managed wood and produces electricity using sustainable energy sources including solar and wind power.

The farm also engages in regenerative agriculture, which entails improving biodiversity, carbon sequestration, and soil health. Cover crops and rotational grazing are used by Shelburne Farms to enhance soil health and lessen erosion. The grazing methods used on the farm also encourage the development of local grasses and wildflowers, which offer habitat for pollinators and other species.

Shelburne Farms excels in environmental education as well. The farm provides a range of educational initiatives and tools for teachers and students, including lesson plans, chances for professional growth, and practical workshops. The educational initiatives at the farm are made to advance environmental literacy, pique interest, and cultivate a love of nature.

information for guests

Shelburne Farms is open all year long and provides a range of events and activities for guests of all ages. 1611 Harbor Road, Shelburne, Vermont 05482 is the address of the farm.

The farm's entrance fee is $10 for adults and $5 for kids aged 3 to 17. Infants and toddlers are free. Discounts are available for groups of ten or more at the farm.

The farm tour and other activities should take at least two hours, according to visitors. As many of the farm's activities take place outside, it is advised to wear comfortable walking shoes and weather-appropriate clothing.

Shelburne Farms holds a number of events throughout the year, including concerts, workshops, and festivals, in addition to its usual activities and tours. A list of forthcoming activities is available on the farm's website for visitors to view.

A famous landmark in Vermont, Shelburne Farms gives tourists a fascinating look at the culture and history of the state's agricultural past. The farm serves as a role model for sustainable agriculture and land use thanks to its dedication to sustainability, environmental education, and community involvement.

Through guided tours, workshops, and educational programs, visitors to Shelburne Farms can learn about cheesemaking, dairy farming, and sustainable agriculture. The farm is a wonderful destination for families, nature enthusiasts, and anybody interested in Vermont's natural marvels because of its stunning landscape, walking paths, and outdoor activities.

CHAPTER FIVE

Vermont`s History & Culture

Vermont`s Covered Bridges

The Green Mountain State, sometimes known as Vermont, is renowned for its breathtaking natural beauty, quaint communities, and extensive history. The covered bridges in Vermont are among the state's most recognizable historical markers. These charming buildings can be found all around the state, and thanks to their distinctive designs and interesting histories, they have become well-known symbols of Vermont culture.

The Origins of Covered Bridges in Vermont

The covered bridge was first built in Vermont in the 19th century, and it is a uniquely American invention. In Vermont, the first covered bridge was constructed in 1820, and by the middle of the nineteenth century, the state had more than 500 of them. The timber trusses in Vermont's covered bridges are shielded from the elements, increasing their lifespan by withstanding the ferocious New England winters.

Covered bridges in Vermont played a significant role in the development of the state's transportation system. They connected villages and cities and made it easier to move people and commodities by allowing passengers to traverse rivers and streams. As a result, many covered bridges were constructed in busy regions, and some of them went on to become well-known icons.

Vermont's various types of covered bridges

There are several different types of covered bridges in Vermont, each with its own distinctive characteristics and background. The Town lattice truss, developed in Vermont in the early 19th century, is the most typical style of covered bridge seen there. The planks are arranged in a crisscross pattern to produce a lattice effect, which gives the bridge stability and support. The Howe truss, the Queen post truss, and the Burr arch truss are other popular styles of covered bridges in Vermont.

The Pulp Mill Covered Bridge in Middlebury is one of Vermont's most well-known covered bridges. One of Vermont's earliest covered bridges, built in 1820, this structure is a prime example of the Town lattice truss style. The neighboring pulp mill that used to be in operation in the area gave its name to the bridge, which has been exquisitely conserved over time.

The West Dummerston Covered Bridge in Dummerston is another remarkable covered bridge in Vermont. This bridge was built in 1872 and has a distinctive lattice truss design with diagonal braces. It is one of the few covered bridges in Vermont that has not undergone major renovations since it was built.

The Covered Bridges in the County of Bennington

Some of Vermont's most stunning covered bridges, each with its own distinct history and allure, can be found in Bennington County. One of the few covered bridges in Vermont that still carries automobile traffic is the Silk Road Covered Bridge in Bennington, which was constructed in 1840. The neighboring Silk Road, which was a well-traveled route for silk traders in the early 19th century, inspired the bridge's name.

The Henry Covered Bridge in Bennington is another well-known covered bridge in the county of Bennington. This bridge was constructed in 1840 and is a prime example of the Town lattice truss construction. It bears the name Henry in honor of the adjacent Henry family, who were early settlers in the region.

One of the rarely-covered bridges in Vermont that have been moved is the Paper Mill Village Covered Bridge in Bennington, which was constructed in 1889. Early in the 20th century, the bridge was shifted to its current site to create room for a new road. It now stands as a tribute to the creativity and resourcefulness of Vermont's bridge builders.

Vermont's Covered Bridges Preservation

Many of Vermont's covered bridges have deteriorated over time, despite their enduring popularity. Many of Vermont's covered bridges have suffered damage from floods, hurricanes, and other natural disasters, and the harsh New England winters can be particularly hard on wooden structures. Additionally, vandalism or arson has been used to destroy some covered bridges.

A Covered Bridge Society has been founded in Vermont to try to safeguard and preserve the state's covered bridges in order to preserve these historic constructions. The society collaborates with neighborhood groups to collect money for bridge restoration and repair projects. It also offers outreach and education initiatives to improve public awareness of the value of Vermont's covered bridges.

People from all over the world have flocked to view Vermont's famous covered bridges as interest in them has recently grown. Many of the covered bridges in the state have been brought back to their former splendor, and they continue to be significant symbols of Vermont's past and present.

The inventiveness, resourcefulness, and dedication to maintaining the state's history and traditions are demonstrated by the covered bridges in Vermont. These famous buildings have endured the test of time, withstanding the hard winters of New England and other natural disasters, and they are still cherished symbols of Vermont culture.

The covered bridges of Vermont will not fail to please you, whether you are a history enthusiast, a wildlife enthusiast, or just seeking a lovely location for your next road trip. Every covered bridge in Vermont has its own beauty and history, from the traditional Town lattice truss to the unusual lattice truss with diagonal braces. So why not visit Vermont and experience these ancient buildings for yourself?

Maple Syrup & Sugar House

The majority of people associate Vermont with maple syrup. The state's culture and history are fundamentally based on sweet, golden syrup. In actuality, Vermont is the US state that produces the most maple syrup. But how did this delectable syrup come to represent the state so strongly? What part do sugarhouses play in making maple syrup, too?

Vermont's History with Maple Syrup

Maple syrup has been produced in Vermont from the beginning of the state's colonization. The first people to harvest maple trees' sweet sap, which they subsequently boiled down to create a syrup, were Native Americans. In the 1600s, European settlers came to the area, and the Native Americans soon taught them the craft of making maple syrup.

The production of maple syrup had grown to be a significant industry in Vermont's economy by the early 1800s. In the spring, farmers would prick their trees, gather the sap in buckets, and boil it down over an open flame. The resulting syrup is used as a sweetener and a cooking ingredient.

New technology made it possible to develop a more effective method of making maple syrup in the middle of the 1800s. The development of a two-part spout and spile system made it possible for sap to flow into a container without the need for ongoing supervision. Farmers were able to tap more trees and make more syrup than ever before because of modern technologies.

Today, Vermont's largest industry is the production of maple syrup. The state is the greatest producer of syrup in the US, producing over one million gallons annually. From pancakes and waffles to baked goods and even drinks, maple syrup is utilized in a wide range of dishes.

The Function of Sugarhouses in the Production of Maple Syrup

In Vermont, the manufacturing of maple syrup relies heavily on sugarhouses. The sap is cooked down in these compact, frequently unassuming facilities to create a syrup. All around the state, sugarhouses can be found on farms and in the woods.

The evaporator in a typical sugarhouse is made of metal or brick and heated by a wood fire. Steam rises from the chimney as the sap boils after being placed into the evaporator. After filtering and bottling, the syrup is prepared for sale.

While many sugarhouses continue to employ this age-old technique, others have embraced contemporary technology. In order to shorten the boiling process and use less fuel, some sugarhouses use reverse osmosis equipment to remove water from the sap before boiling. Others heat their evaporators without using wood, using propane or natural gas instead.

Visiting the Sugarhouses in Vermont

In Vermont, going to a sugarhouse is a well-liked tourist attraction. Many sugarhouses provide tours and tastings so that people can see how maple syrup is made as well as try some of the finished product.

Morse Farm Maple Sugarworks in Montpelier is one of Vermont's most well-known sugarhouses. Since the early 1800s, the farm has been owned by the Morse family for eight generations, and maple syrup has been made there ever since. Visitors are welcome to tour the sugarhouse, taste the syrup, and watch the sap boil in the evaporator.

Palmer's Sugarhouse in Shelburne is another well-known sugarhouse. For more than 50 years, this family-run enterprise has been making maple syrup. Visitors can enjoy a pancake breakfast with fresh syrup while watching the sap being cooked down into syrup.

The history and culture of Vermont are strongly influenced by maple syrup and sugarhouses. The production of maple syrup has played a significant role in shaping the state's character, starting with its origins as a Native American custom and continuing now as a significant industry. Sugarhouses are an essential element of the production process and a well-liked tourist destination thanks to their combination of rustic charm and contemporary technology. Visiting a sugarhouse is a must-do activity when touring Vermont, whether you're a fan of maple syrup or are just interested in the state's culture and history. It's an opportunity to discover the history and methods of making maple syrup, taste some delectable syrup, and become immersed in the state's rich culture and legacy.

Vermont Teddy Bear Factory

Vermont is renowned for its breathtaking natural beauty, quaint communities, and possibilities for outdoor leisure. But the state has a rich cultural and industrial history as well. The Vermont Teddy Bear Factory in Shelburne, Vermont, is one of the most intriguing instances of this. We'll examine the origin, development, and effects on the state of the Vermont Teddy Bear Factory in this chapter as well as its history and culture.

The Vermont Teddy Bear Factory's past

John Sortino started the Vermont Teddy Bear Company in 1981. Sortino created and sold teddy bears out of a cart in Burlington, Vermont, while the company was still a modest operation. But the company quickly gained popularity, and by 1985 Sortino had relocated the business to a bigger location in Shelburne, Vermont. The Vermont Teddy Bear Factory is now a well-known tourist destination in the region, attracting tourists from all over the globe.

The Vermont Teddy Bear Factory's culture

More than just a facility to create teddy bears is the Vermont Teddy Bear Factory. It also reflects the distinct culture and values of the state. The business takes pride in using ethical production techniques and sustainable resources to run a socially responsible enterprise. Many of the bears' accessories and clothing items are made by regional artists and artisans, who are also supported by the factory. From the initial idea to the finishing touches, factory visitors can learn about the creation of a teddy bear. They can also take part in seminars and other events that highlight the business' dedication to innovation and craftsmanship.

The Vermont Teddy Bear Factory's Effects on Vermont

Both culturally and commercially, Vermont has benefited much from the Vermont Teddy Bear Factory. The firm has come to represent Vermont's dedication to sustainable living and moral corporate conduct, and its success has encouraged other companies in the state to do the same. Additionally, the factory provides employment for hundreds of Vermonters, boosting the local economy. Additionally, the factory draws tens of thousands of tourists to the region each year who want to learn about the history of the business and view the process of making teddy bears.

The Vermont Teddy Bear Factory visit

Anyone visiting Vermont should make sure to stop by the Vermont Teddy Bear Factory. The factory offers a variety of experiences and activities, such as factory tours, workshops where bears are made, and a bear hospital where guests may bring their own teddy bears for care. Visitors can buy bears and other items at the factory's retail store. From traditional teddy bears to bears with holiday and special occasion themes, the site offers a huge selection of bears. Additionally, visitors can customize their bears by giving them unique outfits, accessories, and messages.

One-of-a-kind and well-liked institution in Vermont, the Vermont Teddy Bear Factory stands for the state's dedication to creativity, craftsmanship, and sustainability. The state has benefited greatly from the factory's success because it has created jobs and boosted the local economy. A trip to the factory is a great chance to discover Vermont's history and culture and to witness the magic of teddy bear creation firsthand. The Vermont Teddy Bear Factory is a must-visit location whether you're a fan of teddy bears or just curious to learn more about Vermont.

The Von Trapp Family Lodge

Although Vermont is well-known for its beautiful scenery and outdoor activities, it also has a rich cultural and historical heritage that is well worth exploring. The von Trapp Family Lodge, which became internationally famous as the location for the beloved musical film The Sound of Music, is one of Vermont's most well-known cultural icons.

The von Trapp Family's past

A well-known musical family with Austrian roots is the von Trapp clan. Georg von Trapp, the family patriarch, and a decorated naval officer, retired following the conclusion of World War I. Before the start of World War II, the couple had three children from their marriage to Maria Augusta Kutschera, his second wife.

When the von Trapps started appearing together as a family singing group, their musical talent became more apparent. They left Austria in 1938 to avoid the Nazi regime, and they eventually made their way to America. The family carried on performing and touring around the US, achieving recognition and admiration.

The von Trapp family bought a 660-acre farm in Stowe, Vermont, in 1947, and they gave it the name Cor Unum (One Heart). Later, they extended the land, and in 1950, a ski lodge was inaugurated. The von Trapp Family Lodge, which is now a well-known tourist site, was finally created as the family continued to expand over the years.

Lodge of the von Trapp Family

One of the top vacation spots in the state is the von Trapp Family Lodge, which is situated in Stowe, Vermont. The 2,500 acres of land surrounding the resort are home to meadows, woodlands, and breathtaking mountain views. Numerous dining options, a fitness center, a spa, and hiking trails are among the amenities and activities provided by the lodge.

The lodge was initially constructed in the 1950s as a ski lodge, and it has since undergone a number of restorations and additions. The lodge now has 96 guest rooms and suites, each with a distinctive design and allure of its own. Modern conveniences like free Wi-Fi, flat-screen TVs, and plush beds are provided in the rooms.

The von Trapp Family Lodge provides visitors with a number of services and activities in addition to the guest rooms. The lodge offers a tennis court, a fitness center, an outdoor pool, and a hot tub. Additionally, there are more than 30 miles of hiking and biking trails on the property, as well as a working farm where visitors can go see the animals.

The main dining room, the Bierhall, and the bakery are just a few of the dining options available at the lodge. Fine dining is served in the main dining room, with an emphasis on regional and seasonal ingredients. The lodge's brewery and winery's beer and wine are available at the Bierhall, a relaxed dining establishment that welcomes families and serves traditional Austrian cuisine. The bakery sells a selection of freshly baked bread, pastries, and sweets.

The Connection to The Sound of Music

The von Trapp Family Lodge became well-known throughout the world when it served as the model for the iconic musical film The Sound of Music's setting. The von Trapp family's flight from Austria during Nazi occupation is the subject of the 1965 movie.

The von Trapp Family Lodge served as the inspiration for the film's famous opening sequence, even though it wasn't actually used for filming. The surroundings of the lodge and its Austrian-inspired architecture were gorgeous and served as a backdrop. Fans of the movie have started to flock to the lodge to tour the grounds and discover more about the history of the von Trapp family.

Examining the Culture and History of Vermont

One of the many important historical and cultural sites in Vermont is the von Trapp Family Lodge. Many of the state's towns and cities have maintained their historic architecture and cultural traditions, and the state has a long history that dates back to the colonial era.

The Vermont Maple Festival held each spring in the town of St. Albans, is a prominent illustration of Vermont's cultural heritage. The festival incorporates activities including maple syrup tastings, cooking contests, and demonstrations of conventional maple sugaring methods as it honors Vermont's long history of maple syrup production.

The Bennington Museum, which is situated in the town of Bennington, is another significant cultural institution in Vermont. A collection of works by

Vermont artists and artifacts from the state's early inhabitants are among the exhibitions on Vermont's history, art, and culture that can be found at the museum.

There are numerous possibilities to walk, ride, ski, and snowboard in the state's magnificent mountains and forests for people who are interested in discovering Vermont's natural splendor. There are miles of beautiful hiking paths and spectacular panoramas in the state's Green Mountains, which extend from north to south.

Vermont is renowned for its thriving arts and music scene in addition to its stunning natural surroundings. The state hosts a number of annual arts festivals and events, such as the Burlington Discover Jazz Festival, Vermont Symphony Orchestra, and Vermont Shakespeare Festival.

In general, the von Trapp Family Lodge acts as a starting point for discovering Vermont's rich cultural and historical legacy. Every traveler can find something to enjoy in Vermont, whether they want to experience its vibrant arts and music scene, discover the state's natural beauty, or learn about its colonial history. The von Trapp Family Lodge, with its scenic location and first-rate amenities, is the ideal site to begin your Vermont trip.

Vermont Historical Society Museum

The ideal site to delve into the history of the state and discover the individuals who contributed to its current state is the Vermont Historical Society Museum. The museum is housed in a stunning 19th-century structure that was originally the Vermont National Guard headquarters and is situated in Montpelier, the state capital of Vermont. The museum's displays span a wide range of subjects, such as the history of Native Americans in Vermont, colonial Vermont, the Civil War, and contemporary Vermont.

the exhibit on Native Americans

Native Americans have lived in Vermont for almost 10,000 years, and their culture is on display in the museum. Native American groups from Vermont, notably the Abenaki and the Mohawk, have contributed artifacts, tools, and other objects to the exhibition. The culture, customs, and way of life of the tribes, as well as their relationships with European settlers and the effects of colonialism on their societies, are all available for visitors to learn about.

the exhibit on colonial history

The colonial history of Vermont is a significant aspect of the history of the state, which was initially colonized by Europeans in the 17th century. The Colonial History exhibit at the museum spans the era from Vermont's earliest settlement to the American Revolution. Visitors can look at relics from the era, such as tools, furniture, and clothes, and learn about the hardships and victories of early Vermonters.

The Civil War Display

Due to the large number of Vermonters who fought for the Union Army during the Civil War, the state was significantly impacted. The Civil War exhibit at the museum details Vermont's participation in the war, especially the Battle of Gettysburg, where the Vermont Brigade was essential to the Union's triumph. Visitors can view historical objects from the era, such as weaponry, clothing, and private items used by Vermont soldiers.

Contemporary Vermont Exhibition

The Modern-Day Vermont exhibit at the museum spans the years from the Civil War's conclusion to the present. Visitors can discover how Vermont became a contemporary state, including the growth of the small-scale agriculture sector, the ski industry, and the state's dedication to environmental preservation. The exhibition also includes objects from more recent Vermont history, such as relics from the 20th century like vintage clothing and cars.

The Vermont Historical Society Museum offers both temporary and comprehensively diverse exhibits in addition to its permanent ones. Temporary displays recently featured "Vermont Women in the Civil War," "Vermont Photographers: A Survey of the 19th Century," and "The Art of Woodworking in Vermont."

visiting the Museum of the Vermont Historical Society

The hours of operation at the Vermont Historical Society Museum change depending on the season. Adults must pay $7 for admission, elderly and students pay $5, and children under six are admitted free. For school groups and other organizations, the museum also provides group discounts and tailored tours.

Since the museum is in the heart of Montpelier, it is simple to reach from any part of the state. The museum is handicap accessible, and there is plenty of parking close by. The museum's gift shop, which offers a variety of books, trinkets, and items created in Vermont, is also open to visitors.

Anyone interested in the history and culture of the state must pay a visit to the Vermont Historical Society Museum. The museum has something for everyone with its broad selection of exhibits covering everything from Native American history to contemporary Vermont. The Vermont Historical Society Museum is certain to leave a lasting impression and give you a better understanding of Vermont's past and its people, whether you are a history enthusiast, student, or casual visitor. The museum's displays are interesting and instructive, and they include interactive features that make history learning enjoyable and approachable.

The Vermont Historical Society Museum provides a range of educational programs and events year-round in addition to exhibitions. These activities include everything from seminars and workshops to excursions and special events. The museum's enormous library and archives, which are filled with historical details about Vermont and its inhabitants, are also available to visitors.

CHAPTER SIX

Vermont`s Food & Drink Scene

Farm-to-Table Restaurants

Vermont's farm-to-table restaurant culture is equally spectacular as its famed landscapes, maple syrup, and cheese. The state has become a hotspot for locavores, foodies, and everyone who enjoys fine, sustainable cuisine because of its wealth of farms, orchards, and wineries. Vermont offers dining options for every taste and price range, from elegant restaurants to casual eateries.

What does Farm to Table mean?

The "farm-to-table" movement advocates using ingredients that are sustainably produced, in season, and locally obtained. This indicates that the food you eat is freshly produced for you, frequently just hours before it appears on your plate, and comes from farmers and producers in the area. Farm-to-table eateries lessen their carbon footprint and guarantee that their customers receive the freshest, most flavorful food by promoting local agriculture.

Vermont's farm-to-table movement

When a group of regional farmers and food lovers established the Vermont Fresh Network in the 1970s, the farm-to-table movement in Vermont officially got underway. This group encourages the use of regional ingredients in restaurants and other food-related companies by establishing connections between chefs and farmers. Today, Vermont is home to hundreds of farm-to-table eateries, coffee shops, and bakeries, many of which have received accolades for their culinary offerings on a national level.

How to Prepare for a Farm-to-Table Dining Experience

The unpredictability of the menu is one of the pleasures of dining at a farm-to-table establishment. You never know exactly what you'll be eating until you get there since chefs use whatever is in season and readily accessible. But often, you can anticipate foods that highlight the flavors of Vermont's farms and orchards, such as fresh produce, locally sourced meats, and handmade cheeses.

Many farm-to-table restaurants offer extensive drink menus that include regional beers, wines, and spirits in addition to the food. These drinks frequently enhance the flavors of the food and emphasize Vermont's extensive agricultural history.

Try These Farm-to-Table Restaurants

Here are a few eateries to add to your schedule if you're thinking about visiting Vermont and want to sample its farm-to-table cuisine:

Hen of the Wood: Hen of the Wood, with locations in Waterbury and Burlington, is a must-see for foodies. Despite the menu's frequent changes to reflect the seasons, you can always count on unique dishes that showcase Vermont's regional ingredients. Try the artisanal cheeses and the house-made charcuterie.

The Kitchen Table Bistro is a Richmond restaurant that offers traditional New England fare with a farm-to-table touch. Locally produced products are used in dishes such as braised beef short ribs and pan-seared scallops, and Vermont-made beers, wines, and spirits are available on the drink menu.

Ariel's Restaurant is a well-known Brookfield dining establishment that is housed in a gorgeous 19th-century farmhouse. Lamb, hog, and seasonal vegetables are among the ingredients on the weekly changing menu that come from surrounding farms. Dessert must-have: maple crème brulee.

Samuel Pearce Although the hand-blown glassware at this Quechee restaurant is its claim to fame, the food is equally outstanding. Beef farmed in Vermont, trout caught nearby, and fruit from adjacent farms are also on the menu. If you want a truly special dining experience, make sure to reserve a table with a view of the waterfall.

The Red Hen Bakery and Café: In Middlesex, The Red Hen Bakery and Café offers a more relaxed farm-to-table dining experience. The bakery here sells some of the best bread and pastries in the state, and breakfast and lunch are served using organic, locally produced products.

It's vital to be aware that the menu at a farm-to-table restaurant in Vermont can differ from what you're used to. This is so that the recipes would

125

represent the seasonal and local availability of the components, such as fruits, meats, and other items. But this is also one of the things that makes farm-to-table dining such a distinctive and fascinating experience. Although you never know what you'll get, you can be sure that it will be prepared with care and be made with fresh ingredients.

Vermont is home to numerous other farm-to-table eateries, including cafes, bakeries, and even food trucks, in addition to the restaurants mentioned above. To find new favorites and to show support for the numerous farmers, ranchers, and craftspeople who make it all possible, it's worthwhile to explore the local food scene.

The farm-to-table restaurant culture in Vermont is proof of the place's dedication to the environment, the local economy, and fine dining. These restaurants will delight your taste buds and make you feel good about supporting local agriculture, whether you're a foodie or just seeking a fantastic dinner.

Vermont Craft Breweries & Distilleries

Vermont may be a small state, but it holds a significant position in the brewing and distilling industries. With more than 12 refineries and more than 50 bottling plants, Vermont has become a well-known destination for brew and spirits lovers from all over the world. Vermont has it all, from top-notch IPAs to experimental sours and from small-batch gin to award-winning bourbon. In this section, we'll look into Vermont's top breweries and distilleries as well as the unique flavors and styles that make the state's lager and spirits scene so exceptional.

Vermont's specialty brewing

The Vermont Bar and Distillery in Burlington launched the specialty lager scene in Vermont in the 1980s. Since then, it has quickly grown, with additional distilleries opening up all around the state. Specialty distilleries in Vermont are renowned for their commitment to quality, advancement, and sustainability. Many people create interesting and delicious lagers that reflect Vermont's horticultural heritage using privately acquired ingredients like hops, grain, and organic products.

Work is done by Chemist Bottling

The Chemist Bottling Works is perhaps Vermont's most well-known distillery. One of the world's most mind-blowing IPAs is commonly regarded as its flagship beer, Powerful Clincher. Unfiltered, highly aromatic Powerful Clincher has a robust flavor and a silky finish. Other well-known lagers made by The Chemist Brewery include Central Banger, an IPA with fruit and flowers, and Smasher, a refreshing pale beer with citrus overtones. The Chemist Brewery is located in Stowe, and it has a tavern where visitors can sample and buy its lagers.

Mountain Slope Distillery

Another well-known brewery in Vermont is Slope Farmstead Brewery. It is a Greensboro-based establishment renowned for its intricate and delicious beers, a significant portion of which are aged in oak barrels. The extensive range of lagers offered by Slope Farmstead Brewery includes IPAs, stouts, saisons, and sours. Its most well-known lager is perhaps Abner, a deliciously hoppy two-fold IPA that is consistently regarded as among the best beers in the world. Visitors can sample the lagers at Slope Farmstead Brewery's tasting room and buy jugs to take them home.

Fluids by Lawson

A small bottling plant called Lawson's Best Fluids is located in Waitsfield. Its flagship beer, Taste of Daylight, is an IPA that is exceptionally sought after by fans of lager. Other well-known lagers are also provided by Lawson's Best Fluids, including Twofold Daylight, a twofold IPA, and Super Meeting, a meeting IPA. Visitors can sample the distillery's beverages and buy jugs to take them home in the tavern there. Lawson's Best Fluids is renowned for its commitment to sustainability, using locally sourced ingredients and solar-powered energy whenever possible.

Various Reputable Distilleries

Besides the above-mentioned bottling companies, Vermont is home to several other renowned breweries, such as:

- Curve Blending Organization: A tiny Burlington brewery that produces excellent golden beer.
- Burlington Lager Organization: A Williston-based brewery that produces a wide range of experimental and rare lagers.

The Lost Country Preparing Company is a Morrisville-based distillery with experience in producing beers and ales in the Belgian manner.

Shelburne-based Fiddlehead Fermenting Organization is a distillery that makes delicious and intensely hoppy IPAs.

Vermont's creation of spirits

The specialty spirits scene in Vermont may not be as well recognized as the specialty lager scene, but it is just as great. Refineries in Vermont are renowned for their attention to detail and use of local ingredients to produce exceptional and delectable spirits. Everyone can find a favorite in Vermont's specialty spirits scene, which features everything from gin to bourbon to rum to cognac.

Gin Barr Slope

One of Vermont's most well-known spirits is Barr Slope Gin. It is produced by Caledonia Spirits, a Hardwick-based company. A wonderful gin called Barr Slope Gin is given a smooth and sweet flavor by the addition of honey. Additionally, Vermont-sourced juniper and raw honey are used to make the gin. You can enjoy Barr Slope Gin on its own or in a cocktail. Visitors can sample Caledonia

Spirits' libations and learn about the company's refining process in the company's tasting room.

WhistlePig Whiskey

Another renowned Vermont spirit that is provided is WhistlePig Bourbon. WhistlePig Homestead, a refinery in Shoreham, produces it. Rye bourbon WhistlePig Bourbon is aged for at least 10 years in oak barrels. With hints of caramel, vanilla, and zest, it has a flavor that is both rich and complex. In addition, WhistlePig Ranch produces other alcoholic beverages, including whiskey and gin. Visitors can tour the refinery and sample the spirits there.

Waterway Distillers in a hurry

A small distillery called Frantic Waterway Distillers is located in Warren. It supplies a variety of alcoholic beverages, such as rum, bourbon, and cognac. Frantic Waterway Distillers is renowned for its dedication to using local ingredients, such as maple syrup, to create exceptional and delicious spirits. Upheaval Rye, a bourbon with a smooth and zesty flavor that is aged in oak barrels, serves as the drink's main ingredient. Visitors can sample the spirits at Distraught Stream Distillers' tasting room and learn more about the refining process there.

Other Provocative Refineries

Besides the refineries mentioned above, Vermont is home to several other excellent refineries, such as:

Runners' Score Refinery: A distillery in Jeffersonville that uses grains and botanicals that are procured privately to make vodka, gin, and bourbon.

Middlebury-based Stonecutter Spirits is a distillery that uses local water and grains to create gin and bourbon.

Middlebury-based Appalachian Hole Refinery produces a variety of alcoholic beverages, such as gin, vodka, and cognac.

There is something for everyone in Vermont's specialty brew and spirits sector, which is diverse and vibrant. Vermont offers a wide range of options to explore, regardless of your preference for beer or for spirits. From outstanding IPAs to unique gins, and award-winning bourbons to experimental sours, Vermont's bottling works and refineries are producing some of the best art libations in the world. So raise a glass or 16 ounces in celebration of Vermont's delectable food and beverage scene!

Cabot Cheese Factory

Vermont is renowned for its breathtaking natural beauty, quaint communities, and kind residents. But the state is also well-known for its culinary and beverage offerings, with a focus on artisanal and locally made goods. The Cabot Cheese Factory, which offers tours and tastings that highlight some of the best dairy products in the state, is one of Vermont's most well-known tourist attractions for foodies.

Cabot Creamery's past

A group of dairy farmers in Cabot, Vermont, came together in 1919 to form a cooperative so they could pool their resources and increase their earnings. This is how Cabot Creamery got its start. Farmers in the cooperative produced some of the best dairy goods in the area, and the cooperative grew and prospered over time. Farmers still control Cabot Creamery today, and the company is dedicated to creating high-quality goods while promoting regional agriculture and sustainable business practices.

the Cabot Cheese Factory tours

A visit to the Cabot Cheese Factory in Vermont is a must-do if you enjoy cheese. The plant is situated in Cabot, a small community in the northeastern region of the state, and it provides daily tours that walk guests through the entire process of creating cheese.

The tours begin with a brief movie that provides an overview of Cabot Creamery's history and the manufacturing of cheese. Then, after being shown around the factory, visitors can see how cheese is made using raw milk that is obtained from nearby dairy farms.

The observation room, where visitors can observe cheese being cut and wrapped for export, is one of the tour's highlights. Large windows in the area enable guests to observe the entire procedure, and the aroma of freshly made cheese permeates the space.

Cabot Cheese Factory tastings

Visitors can try some of the excellent cheese produced on-site after the tour. Visitors are welcome to sample as many cheeses as they would like at the Cabot Cheese Factory, which provides everything from mild cheddar to pungent blues.

The Seriously Sharp Cheddar, which has received multiple honors and is recognized for its tangy flavor and creamy texture, is one of the most well-liked cheeses at the Cabot Cheese Factory. The Pepper Jack, Habanero, and Vermont Sharp White Cheddar are some further well-liked cheeses.

The Cabot Cheese Factory also sells additional dairy items like butter, yogurt, and sour cream in addition to cheese. Visitors are able to try these goods as well as buy their favorites to take home.

the Cabot Cheese Factory tour

Year-round hours of operation for the Cabot Cheese Factory include daily visits from 9 am to 4 pm. Although there is no cost for the tours, donations are welcome to support regional agriculture and sustainable practices.

Be cautious to dress comfortably when visiting the Cabot Cheese Factory because the environment might be chilly and damp. As the tours can last up to an hour, be ready to walk and stand for extended periods of time.

Last but not least, don't forget to bring some food! The tastings at the Cabot Cheese Factory, which sells some of the best cheeses and dairy goods in the area, are a highlight of any trip there. Therefore, make sure to indulge in as many samples as you like and bring some of your favorites home to enjoy later.

If you love cheese or are a foodie, you must visit the Cabot Cheese Factory while you are in Vermont. The tastings are delectable and fulfilling, and the excursions are educational and amusing. So when you're visiting Vermont's food and beverage scene, make sure to include a visit to the Cabot Cheese Factory on your schedule. You won't be let down!

Farmer`s Market & Local Produce

Vermont is renowned for its beautiful scenery, quaint communities, and possibilities for outdoor leisure. But it's also a haven for foodies, with a thriving culinary scene that highlights regional dairy, artisanal goods, and produce. We will examine Vermont's farmer's markets, fresh produce, and the thriving food and drink scene they have sparked in this section.

Markets for produce

Farmers' markets have a long history in Vermont. Farmers, growers, and craftspeople congregate there to sell their wares and interact with the local population. Fresh produce, meat, dairy, baked goods, crafts, and other things are all available at the markets. They serve as a focal point for various neighborhood events, food trucks, and live music. The following are some of Vermont's best farmer's markets:

Burlington Farmers Market: With over 90 merchants selling a range of fresh produce, prepared dishes, and crafts, the Burlington Farmers Market is the biggest in Vermont. The market is situated in the center of downtown Burlington and is open every Saturday from May through October.

Montpelier Farmers Market: From May to October, a bustling market is held every Saturday in Montpelier. Visitors can take in the lovely settings while enjoying fresh vegetables, cooked dishes, and crafts at this location on the State House lawn.

Rutland Farmers Market: Open all year round, the Rutland Farmers Market provides a wide range of fresh fruit, baked goods, meats, and artisanal crafts. On Saturdays, while the market is open, visitors can take in live music performances and other neighborhood activities.

Stowe Farmers Market: From May to October, the Stowe Farmers Market is a well-liked market that is open every Sunday. Visitors can also take in live music performances and other neighborhood events, in addition to a wide selection of fresh fruit, prepared dishes, and crafts.

regional food

Locally grown food is king in Vermont's culinary landscape. Several different types of crops, including apples, berries, vegetables, and maple syrup, are produced by the state's thriving farming community. The best restaurants in the state frequently use fresh, in-season, and tasty ingredients that come from nearby farmers and suppliers.

Maple syrup is among the most recognizable products from Vermont. In the United States, Vermont is the state that produces the most maple syrup, which is utilized in a wide range of foods and beverages. In every part of the state, restaurants, sugarhouses, and farmer's markets provide samples of maple syrup.

Cheese is yet another regional item for which Vermont is renowned. Dairy farming has a long history in the state, and many of its best cheesemakers create award-winning cheeses that are offered at farmer's markets, specialty shops, and eateries. Additionally, visitors can sample various kinds of cheese while touring the production facilities.

Also well known for its apple orchards in Vermont. A wide variety of apples, including heirloom types that are unique to the state, are available. In orchards all over the state, visitors can choose their own apples, and many farmer's markets also sell freshly made apple goods like cider, pies, and donuts.

Craft Wine, Spirits, and Beer

Local ingredients are simply one aspect of Vermont's food and beverage landscape. The craft wine, beer, and spirits industries are all growing in this state. Over 50 craft breweries can be found in Vermont, including some of the best in the nation.

Many of the breweries offer tours of the facilities, beer flights for tasting, and food pairings.

There are numerous wineries and distilleries in Vermont. Many of these producers make their unique and flavorful beverages using local fruits and grains. Visitors are welcome to sample the vineyards' wines, spirits, and creative cocktails while on tours of the distilleries. Shelburne Vineyard, Boyden Valley Winery, and Lincoln Peak Vineyard are a few of Vermont's most well-known vineyards. Visitors interested in spirits might check out the Vermont Spirits Distilling Company, which creates a range of alcoholic beverages, such as vodka, gin, and whiskey.

Farm-to-Table Dining

The pinnacle of the state's dining and drinking scene is found in Vermont's farm-to-table establishments. These eateries create inventive and delectable dishes using the finest artisanal and local ingredients from Vermont. The majority of Vermont's farm-to-table eateries closely collaborate with regional farmers and producers to acquire their ingredients, ensuring that the cuisine is healthy, sustainable, and beneficial to the community.

The Kitchen Table Bistro in Richmond is one of Vermont's most well-known farm-to-table eateries. The restaurant's menu is constantly changing to take seasonality and the availability of nearby ingredients into account. Hen of the Wood, a prominent farm-to-table eatery with locations in Waterbury and Burlington, is another. The menu at the eatery emphasizes Vermont characteristics with dishes including grilled venison, roasted beets, and maple crème brûlée.

The state's thriving farming community, handcrafted goods, and local produce are all celebrated in Vermont's food and beverage industry. The farmer's markets serve as a focal point for neighborhood activities and a display of the state's wide range of agricultural goods. Visitors can enjoy tours of wineries, distilleries, and craft breweries while sampling the finest locally produced foods, such as maple syrup, cheese, and apples, from Vermont. The farm-to-table eateries use the freshest local ingredients available to craft inventive and delectable dishes. There is something for everyone in this charming New England state, whether you're a foodie or just interested in learning more about Vermont's culinary industry.

Vermont Specialty Food

Vermont is a small state with a significant reputation in the food and beverage industry. Vermont, which is well-known for its maple syrup, cheddar, and specialty brew, has a unique culinary culture that reflects its rural heritage and commitment to sustainability.

We'll look into some of Vermont's most infamous specialty food sources in this chapter, including apple juice and maple sugar. From there, the possibilities are endless. We'll also delve into the history and traditions behind each food, as well as suggest a few locations where you may sample these mouthwatering sweets.

adzuna syrup

Perhaps no food has a stronger association with Vermont than maple syrup. Since Native Americans previously demonstrated how to manufacture it too early settlers, maple syrup has been produced in Vermont by tapping maple trees and collecting their sap.

Today, Vermont produces more than 40% of all US maple syrup, making it the largest producer in the country. The traditional maple syrup season lasts from February to April when the temperature warms and the sap begins to flow.

In Vermont, you may find maple syrup in a variety of forms, including traditional glass jars, maple candies, sweets, and even espresso with a maple flavor. The Morse Homestead Maple Sugarworks in Montpelier, the Cabot Creamery Extension in Waterbury, and the Bragg Ranch Sugarhouse and Gift Shop in East Montpelier are among the most well-known places to taste maple syrup in Vermont.

Cheddar

Cheddar is another cuisine that has a strong connection to Vermont. Since the middle of the 19th century, when dairy producers began moving to Vermont to protect their surplus milk, cheddar has been made there using cow's milk.

Vermont cheddar is now highly regarded for its opulent, tangy flavor, and velvety surface. Many of Vermont's cheddar producers still use traditional methods to deliver their product, such as hand-going and cave-aging it to ensure even flavor distribution.

The Cabot Creamery Addition in Waterbury, the Grafton Town Cheddar Organization in Grafton, and the Shelburne Homesteads Ranch Store in Shelburne are among the most well-known locations to sample Vermont cheddar.

Pear Juice

Another famous specialty cuisine worth seeking out is Vermont's apple juice. Vermont apple juice, which is made from freshly squeezed apples and is revitalizing, sweet, and fresh, is a well-known beverage in the fall.

Many farms and plantations in Vermont make their own apple juice, which can be found in ranchers' stores and ranch remains all over the state. The Blissful Valley Plantation in Middlebury, the Chapin Plantation in Essex, and the Virus Empty Juice Plant in Waterbury are among the most well-known locations to sample Vermont apple juice.

Maple Syrup

If you have a sweet tooth, be sure to try some candy made with Vermont maple syrup. Maple candy is a lustful delight that will definitely gratify your cravings. It is made by heating maple syrup to a high temperature and then pouring it into molds.

Many Vermont maple syrup producers also produce maple candy, which is sold in rancher's markets, gift shops, and specialty food stores all over the state. The Morse Homestead Maple Sugarworks in Montpelier, the Virus Empty Juice Factory in Waterbury, and the Lake Champlain Chocolates Processing and Store in Burlington are the three most well-known locations to sample Vermont maple candy.

Particular Brew

Finally, a discussion of Vermont's food and beverage scene would not be complete without mentioning specialty brew. In Vermont, there are more than 50 art bottlers, several of which produce award-winning lagers that are highly sought after by beer enthusiasts.

The Chemist Bottling Works for Stowe, Slope Farmstead Distillery in Greensboro, and Lawson's Best Fluids in Waitsfield are probably the most well-known specialty breweries in Vermont.

Every distillery has a distinct aesthetic, and many provide tours and tastings so you can see how their drink is prepared.

Vermont's specialty lager scene is renowned for emphasizing local ingredients and practicing blending techniques. Many bottling operations use grains and bounce from Vermont, and some even have their own homesteads where they grow their own ingredients. Numerous breweries also put an emphasis on lowering waste and minimizing their environmental impact.

In Vermont, IPAs, stouts, and bitter lagers are the three most popular beer types. In addition, the state is renowned for its seasonal brews, such as fruity brews in the late spring and pumpkin and maple lagers in the fall.

Whether you enjoy a lager or simply want to try something new, Vermont's specialty brew culture is well worth exploring.

Other sources of specialty foods

While some of Vermont's most well-known specialty food producers include maple syrup, cheddar, apple juice, maple candy, and specialty brew, there are many other delectable treats to be found as well.

One example is the honey from Vermont, which is distributed by local beekeepers using honey bees that collect nectar from wildflowers, clover, and other plants. Vermont honey is renowned for its distinctive flavor and aroma, which can vary depending on the season and the flowering season.

Fudge is another unique dish to try in Vermont. Fudge is a rich and generous delicacy that comes in a variety of flavors. It is made by combining sugar, spread, cream, and other ingredients. The Vermont Fudge Manufacturing Company in Ludlow and the Stowe Fudge Organization in Stowe are two of Vermont's most well-known fudge stores.

Vermont is renowned for its excellent bread, which is produced by local dough punchers using traditional methods and ingredients that are purchased privately. Red Hen Baking Company in Middlesex and O Bread Pastry Kitchen in Shelburne are two well-known bakeries to try.

Finally, Vermont's ranchers' business sectors are a fantastic place to find a variety of specialty food sources, from fresh produce and jams made just for you to unique cheeses and heated goods. The Burlington Ranchers' Market, the Montpelier Ranchers' Market, and the Rutland Ranchers' Market are a few well-known ranchers' business sectors in Vermont. Vermont's food and drink scene is an impression of its rural roots, obligation to sustainability, and commitment to using privately obtained fixings. In Vermont, you may get a wide variety of delectable specialized food products, such as maple syrup and cheddar, apple juice, maple sweets, and specialty lager, and that's only the beginning.

Whether you're a foodie looking to learn more about Vermont's culinary tradition or just looking for a tasty treat to enjoy, be sure to try some of the state's well-known specialized food sources while you're there.

CHAPTER SEVEN

Outdoor Activities

Hiking & Camping in the Green Mountain

Outdoor enthusiasts, especially those who enjoy hiking and camping, will find Vermont to be a haven. The best area to discover the grandeur of Vermont's natural sceneries is in the Green Mountains, a mountain range that stretches from the Canadian border to the Massachusetts state boundary. We'll explore the top hiking and camping areas in the Green Mountains in this chapter, as well as what makes them unique.

the Green Mountains hiking

There are hundreds of miles of hiking paths in the Green Mountains, from simple, leisurely strolls for families to strenuous multi-day backpacking excursions. Here are a few of the Green Mountains' most well-liked hiking routes.

lengthy trail

The 273-mile Long Trail, which connects the Canadian and Massachusetts borders, is Vermont's most famous hiking route. The trail offers breathtaking views of the valleys and peaks in the area as it travels along the spine of the Green Mountains. Hikers have the option of taking on the full trail at once or exploring smaller segments.

Mansfield Mountain

The tallest peak in Vermont is called Mount Mansfield, and it is 4,393 feet high. There are many trails that can be used by hikers to get to the peak, including the well-liked Sunset Ridge Trail and the difficult Hell Brook Trail. Hikers are rewarded with expansive views of the neighboring mountains once they reach the summit.

the Camel's Hump

Another well-liked hiking location in the Green Mountains is Camel's Hump. With a height of 4,083 feet, the peak provides a 360-degree view of the mountains and forests in the area. The most well-known ascent path is the Monroe Trail.

Alps to Coast Trail

The Appalachian Trail travels 100 miles from Massachusetts to Norwich, Vermont, across the Green Mountains. The trail is a well-liked destination for day hikers and thru-hikers alike since it offers a range of scenery, from rough mountains to gentle hills.

In the Green Mountains, tent camping

In the Green Mountains, camping is a well-liked hobby. Campgrounds range from basic wilderness sites to RV parks with full hookups. Here are a few of the top Green Mountains camping locations.

National Forest of Green Mountain

There are numerous campgrounds located inside Vermont's Green Mountain National Forest, which spans more than 400,000 acres. The majority of the campgrounds are situated close to hiking trails or on picturesque byways, giving them the ideal starting point for outdoor pursuits.

Dunmore Lake

Many campgrounds are situated on the lake's shore, making Lake Dunmore a well-liked camping location in the Green Mountains. The nearby forests include several hiking and bike paths, and the lake is ideal for swimming, boating, and fishing.

State Park at Gifford Woods

Near Killington, Gifford Woods State Park has more than 50 campsites. The park has easy access to hiking trails and streams for fishing and is encircled by the verdant forests of the Green Mountains.

State Park Molly Stark

Over 20 campsites are available at Molly Stark State Park, which is situated in the southern Green Mountains. The park, which has a number of hiking routes and picnic spots, is named for the spouse of American Revolutionary War general John Stark.

How to Camp and Hike in the Green Mountains

In advance: Plan your hiking or camping excursion accordingly after conducting an appropriate study on the location you'll be visiting. Know the trail's complexity, the current weather, and whether any reservations or permits are required.

Pack sensibly: Make sure you include sufficient water, food, and weather- and terrain-appropriate clothing and equipment. Keep important items like a map, compass, and first aid kit close at hand.

Remove all traces: Pack out all garbage and leave the campsite or path in a clean, pristine condition as a sign of your respect for the environment. Follow any rules and regulations pertaining to campfires and waste disposal, and avoid harming flora or wildlife.

Observe wildlife: Black bears, moose, and coyotes are among the many species of fauna that call the Green Mountains home. To prevent attracting wildlife, store your food and trash appropriately. Also, be prepared to handle wildlife you come across on the route.

Regarding other campers and hikers: The Green Mountains are a well-liked vacation spot, especially in the summer. Be considerate to other campers and hikers by minimizing noise and giving them space.

Be ready for emergencies: Have a plan in place and know how to call emergency services in case of an emergency. Bring a phone that is fully charged or bring another form of communication, and tell someone about your plans and the time you plan to return.

Any outdoor enthusiast visiting Vermont must go hiking and camping in the Green Mountains. The Green Mountains provide countless options for adventure and exploration thanks to their extensive network of hiking paths, picturesque campgrounds, and breathtaking natural settings. There is a path and campground to meet your needs, whether you're an expert hiker or a novice. You may be sure to have a wonderful experience in Vermont's Green Mountains as long as you prepare ahead of time, pack wisely, and show respect for the surrounding area and other tourists.

Skiing & Snowboarding in the Winter

Vermont is a winter wonderland, with pristine snow-covered mountains, picturesque ski resorts, and a long history of skiing and snowboarding. Vermont offers some of the best skiing and snowboarding experiences in the country, whether you're an expert skier or a novice.

In this chapter, we'll explore the top ski resorts in Vermont, the best skiing and snowboarding trails, and everything else you need to know to have an unforgettable winter vacation in Vermont.

Vermont Ski Resorts

Vermont is home to some of the most popular and prestigious ski resorts in the United States, such as Stowe Mountain Resort, Killington Resort, and Stratton Mountain Resort. These resorts are appropriate for skiers and snowboarders of all skill levels because they offer everything from easy slopes to challenging terrain.

Stowe Mountain Resort: Stowe Mountain Resort is one of the most popular ski resorts in Vermont, offering over 4,000 acres of skiable terrain. With its varied terrain and stunning views of Mount Mansfield, Stowe Mountain Resort is an excellent choice for both beginners and experienced skiers.

Killington Resort: Killington Resort is the largest ski resort in the eastern United States, with over 1,500 acres of skiable terrain. The resort offers a range of terrain, including beginner slopes, intermediate trails, and challenging expert terrain. Killington also has one of the longest ski seasons in the region, making it a popular choice for skiers and snowboarders.

Stratton Mountain Resort: Stratton Mountain Resort is known for its excellent grooming and diverse terrain, including beginner slopes, intermediate trails, and challenging expert terrain. Along with these activities, the resort provides snowmobiling, ice skating, and snowshoeing.

Mount Snow: Mount Snow is located in the southern part of Vermont and offers a wide range of terrain for skiers and snowboarders of all levels. The resort also has a state-of-the-art terrain park, making it a popular choice for freestyle skiers and snowboarders.

Okemo Mountain Resort: Okemo Mountain Resort is located in Ludlow, Vermont, and offers over 600 acres of skiable terrain. The resort also offers a range of activities, including snow tubing, ice skating, and snowshoeing.

Best Skiing and Snowboarding Trails

Vermont offers some of the best skiing and snowboarding trails in the United States. There are several trails to select from, regardless of your level of experience.

Beginner Trails

If you're new to skiing or snowboarding, Vermont has plenty of beginner-friendly trails to help you get started. Here are some of the best beginner trails in Vermont:

Bear Cub: Bear Cub is a gentle, wide-open trail at Killington Resort, making it an excellent choice for beginners.

Liftline: Liftline is a gentle beginner trail at Stowe Mountain Resort, offering stunning views of Mount Mansfield.

Easy Street: Easy Street is a beginner trail at Okemo Mountain Resort, offering gentle terrain for those just starting out.

Intermediate Trails

Intermediate trails in Vermont offer a bit more challenge, making them perfect for those looking to improve their skills. Here are some of the best intermediate trails in Vermont:

Northway: Northway is a popular intermediate trail at Stowe Mountain Resort, offering varied terrain and stunning views.

Great Eastern: Great Eastern is a long, winding intermediate trail at Killington Resort, offering challenging terrain and stunning views.

Wanderer: Wanderer is an intermediate trail at Stratton Mountain Resort, offering varied terrain and stunning views.

Expert Trails

Expert routes in Vermont feature some of the most demanding terrains in the United States, making them appropriate for expert skiers and snowboarders. Here are some of the best expert trails in Vermont:

Goat: Goat is a tough expert trail at Stowe Mountain Resort, notable for its steep slopes and moguls.

Outer Limits: Outer Limits is a tough expert course at Killington Resort, known for its steep, tight terrain and challenging moguls.

Upper FIS: Upper FIS is a tough expert course at Stratton Mountain Resort, notable for its steep slopes and limited terrain.

Other Activities

In addition to skiing and snowboarding, Vermont provides a number of other winter sports. Here are some of the most popular activities to try during your winter vacation in Vermont:

Snowshoeing: Snowshoeing is a terrific way to enjoy Vermont's winter countryside. Many ski resorts offer snowshoe rentals and guided tours.

Ice Skating: Vermont boasts several outdoor ice skating rinks, including the popular rink at The Essex Resort & Spa.

Snowmobiling: Snowmobiling is a fantastic way to experience Vermont's snow-covered terrain. Many ski resorts offer snowmobile rentals and guided tours.

Sleigh Rides: Sleigh rides are a delightful way to discover Vermont's winter countryside. Many ski resorts offer sleigh ride tours, complete with blankets and hot cocoa.

With some of the best skiing and snowboarding in the country, Vermont is a winter wonderland. The ski resorts in Vermont have something to offer skiers of all skill levels. Snowshoeing and sleigh rides are only a couple of the numerous winter sports available besides skiing and snowboarding. Make plans for your winter getaway to Vermont right away to take in its allure.

Biking & Cycling

Vermont is a state renowned for its magnificent scenery and natural beauty, making it the ideal vacation spot for outdoor enthusiasts. Cycling and riding are common pastimes in Vermont due to the state's kilometers of beautiful roads and trails. Every type of biker will find a journey that suits them, whether they prefer leisurely rides through quaint towns or technical mountain biking paths. We'll look at some of Vermont's top bike and cycling routes in this chapter.

The Champlain Bicycle Path

The 363-mile Champlain Bikeway encircles Lake Champlain and provides stunning views of the Adirondacks and the Green Mountains. The bikeway is appropriate for bikers of all skill levels because it is made up primarily of paved roads with some off-road sections. Middlebury, Burlington, and Vergennes are just a few of the picturesque towns and villages that the route travels through. Bicyclists can refuel and rest at nearby breweries, eateries, and farmers' markets along the route.

Trails of The Kingdom

A network of more than 100 miles of mountain bike trails is called The Kingdom Trails, and it is situated in Vermont's Northeast Kingdom. All mountain biker skill levels, from beginners to experts, can use the trails. The paths are well-maintained and clearly marked thanks to the Kingdom Paths Association. The trails offer breathtaking views of the surroundings as they wind through thick forests, undulating hills, and through streams.

The recreation trail in Stowe

A 5.3-mile paved walkway called the Stowe Recreation Walkway winds through the picturesque village of Stowe. All levels of bikers, including families with children, can use the path. The route traverses wide fields, woodlands, and bridges as it follows the West Branch River. Bicyclists can pause at a number of picnic spots, breathtaking vistas, and swimming holes along the route.

Trail of the Island Line

The eastern edge of Lake Champlain is bordered by the 14-mile Island Line Trail. The Adirondack Mountains and the lake are beautifully visible from the route. The Colchester Causeway, a short sliver of land jutting into the lake, is where the trail comes to an end after starting in Burlington. Cyclists can cross the causeway while taking in the expansive vistas of the lake on either side.

Valley of the Mad River

There are many beautiful roads and paths to select from in the Mad River Valley, making it a well-liked location for bikers. The Green Mountains encircle the valley, providing breathtaking views of the peaks and valleys. Numerous routes are available for cyclists, including the 3.8-mile paved Mad River Path that runs through the towns of Waitsfield and Warren. Cycling enthusiasts can explore the mountainous dirt roads and trails for more difficult routes.

the bike path in Burlington

The 7.5-mile-long paved Burlington Bike Path follows Lake Champlain's shoreline. The Adirondack Mountains and the lake are beautifully visible from the path. Several parks, including Oakledge Park, Battery Park, and Waterfront Park, are traversed by the path. Bicyclists can pause at a number of eateries, cafes, and stores along the route.

Trail of the Catamount

The 300-mile Catamount Trail spans Vermont's whole length, from the Massachusetts border to the Canadian border. The year-round trail is appropriate for mountain biking, hiking, and skiing. The Green Mountains are traversed by the path, which provides breathtaking views of their peaks and valleys. There are various trail segments available for cyclists, ranging in difficulty from moderate to difficult.

The Greenway in Burlington

The 7.5-mile Burlington Greenway is a paved path that follows the city's waterfront. Beautiful views of Lake Champlain and the Adirondack Mountains may be seen from the walkway. The route is popular with both locals and visitors and is appropriate for cyclists of all skill levels. Several parks, including Waterfront Park and North Beach Park, where there are many opportunities for swimming, picnicking, and other recreational activities, are traversed by the path.

Railway in the Lamoille Valley

Northern Vermont's picturesque Lamoille Valley is traversed by the 93-mile Lamoille Valley Rail Trail. The trail offers breathtaking views of the surrounding countryside as it travels along an old railroad bed. The trail is open all year long and is appropriate for cyclists of all skill levels. Bicyclists can pause along the road in a number of tiny towns and villages, like Johnson and Morrisville, and make use of the cafes and stores there.

The Mountain Bike Trails in Bolton Valley

In the Green Mountains next to Bolton Valley Resort, there is a network of more than 100 miles of mountain riding routes known as the Bolton Valley Mountain Bike Routes. All mountain biker skill levels, from beginners to experts, can use the trails. The trails offer breathtaking views of the surroundings as they wind through thick forests, undulating hills, and through streams. Cycling enthusiasts have a variety of options, from straightforward courses suitable for families to more difficult trails suitable for experts.

Guidelines for Cycling and Biking in Vermont

Get Ready: The weather in Vermont can be erratic, so make sure to pack clothes for every situation. Bring lots of water, food, and sunscreen, too.

Know the Law: Because Vermont's roads can be congested and twisty, it's crucial to abide by the law and pay attention to other traffic. If cycling at night, always use a helmet, lights, and reflectors.

Respect the Environment: Vermont is renowned for its stunning natural surroundings, so it's crucial to do your part to preserve it and leave no mark. Stay on designated trails and remove all trash.

Before setting out, make cautious to verify the trail conditions because the weather and other factors can have an impact on Vermont's trails.

A distinctive and immersive approach to appreciating Vermont's natural beauty and charm is biking and cycling. There are many routes and trails to discover, whether you are an experienced biker or a novice. The varied environment of Vermont has something for everyone, from the challenging mountain bike trails of the Northeast Kingdom to the picturesque roads along Lake Champlain. So get on your bike, load it up, and head out to see Vermont from the comfort of your bike.

Kayaking, Canoeing, & Paddleboarding

The state of Vermont is well-known for its breathtaking natural scenery and plenty of outdoor activities. One of Vermont's most well-liked vacation spots for outdoor enthusiasts is Lake Champlain. The 120-mile-long lake has borders with Vermont, New York, and Quebec. Kayaking, canoeing, and paddleboarding are all ideal here.

A great place to go kayaking, canoeing, and paddleboarding is Lake Champlain, which has a number of islands, bays, and inlets. It is simple to understand why so many people travel to Lake Champlain for outdoor sports given the lake's crystal-clear water and breathtaking scenery. We'll look at some of the best spots on Lake Champlain to kayak, canoe, and paddleboard in this chapter.

Lake Champlain kayaking

Lake Champlain may be explored well by kayak. If you own a kayak, you can launch it from one of the many public access points around the lake. Kayaks can be rented from a number of locations. The Burlington Waterfront is one of the most popular locations for kayaking on Lake Champlain. The 7.5-mile-long Burlington Waterfront is a cycling path that follows Lake Champlain's shoreline. At Waterfront Park, you can paddle around the lake in a kayak from the beach.

North Hero State Park is yet another well-liked location for kayaking on Lake Champlain. The park has a beach area where you may launch your kayak as well as a boat launch. From there, you can tour the lake's numerous islands and inlets. Additionally, you can paddle to the Alburgh Dunes State Park, a wonderful location for swimming and picnicking.

Try paddling around the Four Brothers Islands if you want a kayaking adventure that is more difficult. Four islands collectively known as the Four Brothers Islands are situated in the center of Lake Champlain. They are a well-liked location for kayakers due to the difficult currents and breathtaking scenery.

Lake Champlain canoeing

Another well-liked pastime on Lake Champlain is canoeing. If you own a canoe, you can launch it from one of the many public access locations all around the lake. They're numerous places where you can hire canoes. The Missisquoi National Wildlife Refuge on Lake Champlain is one of the most well-liked locations for canoeing. The Missisquoi River and Dead Creek are only two of the canoe-friendly streams in the refuge.

The LaPlatte River is another well-liked location for canoeing on Lake Champlain. The LaPlatte River flows into Lake Champlain at a modest rate.

As a result of the tranquil waterways and breathtaking scenery, it's an excellent place for canoeing.

Try canoeing through the Lamoille River if you want a more difficult canoeing experience. The Lamoille River is a swift-moving river that presents skilled canoeists with some difficult rapids.

Lake Champlain paddleboarding

Lake Champlain paddleboarding is a relatively new hobby, but it has already gained popularity as a popular way to explore the lake. If you own a paddleboard, you can launch it from one of the many public access points around the lake. Paddleboards can be rented from a number of locations. The Burlington Waterfront is one of the most well-liked locations to paddleboard on Lake Champlain. It's an excellent place for novices because of the tranquil seas and breathtaking scenery.

Oakledge Park is another well-liked location for paddleboarding on Lake Champlain. You can paddleboard in the park's beach area and explore the lake from there. The park also features a number of hiking routes with breathtaking lake views.

Try paddling to Mallctts Bay if you want a more difficult paddleboarding experience. A sizable harbor called Mallett's Harbor can be found in Lake Champlain's northern region. The area contains a number of tiny islands and coves that are ideal for paddleboarding exploration. Before attempting to paddle in the bay, it's vital to have some previous paddleboarding expertise due to the bay's tough currents.

Lake Champlain Kayaking, Canoeing, and Paddleboarding Safety Tips

The following safety advice should be kept in mind before kayaking, canoeing, or paddleboarding on Lake Champlain to guarantee a fun and safe experience:

- Put on a life vest: Regardless of your degree of skill or the weather, always wear a life jacket.
- The weather, please: Check the weather forecast before leaving to make sure there aren't any storms or strong winds expected.

- Bring a map: It's important to know the local waterways and currents and to have a map of the area with you.
- Bring a whistle; in an emergency, it can be used to call for assistance.
- Stick close to the shore: If you're a beginner or the conditions aren't the best, stick close to the shore.
- Keep yourself hydrated by packing plenty of water and energy foods.
- Beware of motorboats: Be mindful of motorboats at all times and allow them the right of way.

Kayaking, canoeing, and paddleboarding are wonderful activities that may be enjoyed on Lake Champlain. It is understandable why so many outdoor enthusiasts choose Lake Champlain for their activities given the lake's crystal-clear waters and breathtaking scenery. On Lake Champlain, there is something for everyone, from the serene waters of the Burlington Waterfront to the strenuous currents of the Four Brothers Islands. Just keep in mind to heed the safety advice to guarantee a fun and secure encounter. Enjoy your paddling!

Fishing & Hunting

The state of Vermont is renowned for its breathtaking natural beauty, which includes its clear lakes, lush forests, and undulating hills. It's a heaven for outdoor enthusiasts, offering a variety of recreational activities like fishing and hunting.

Lake fishing in Vermont

Anglers flock to Vermont because its lakes and rivers are home to a wide variety of fish species, including trout, bass, perch, pike, and walleye. The Connecticut River, the Battenkill River, and Lake Champlain are a few of Vermont's most well-liked fishing locations.

More than 90 different fish species, including landlocked salmon, lake trout, and bass, can be found in Lake Champlain, the sixth-largest freshwater lake in the United States. Additionally, the lake hosts a number of fishing competitions throughout the year that draw anglers from all over the world.

Another well-liked spot for fishing, particularly for trout and salmon, is the Connecticut River, which runs along the border between Vermont and New Hampshire. Because of the river's famed natural

171

beauty, fishermen can enjoy a day on the water there.

Fly fishing aficionados frequently travel to the Battenkill River, which flows through southwest Vermont. The river is a great place to capture brown trout, rainbow trout, and brook trout because it is their natural habitat.

A fishing license must be obtained before going fishing in Vermont. This can be done online or at a number of retail stores spread out across the state. Hunting in Vermont's Forests The Vermont Fish & Wildlife Department also has a variety of rules and restrictions in place to guarantee the survival of fish populations.

Due to the abundance of wildlife in its forests, Vermont is a well-liked hunting destination. Numerous species, including deer, moose, bear, turkey, and waterfowl, are huntable in the state.

White-tailed deer thrive in Vermont's numerous forests and fields, which makes deer shooting there extremely popular. Regulated hunting is used by the Vermont Fish & Wildlife Department to control the state's deer population, helping to preserve healthy deer herds and offering hunters a recreational option.

Another well-liked pastime in Vermont is moose hunting, for which the state issues a set number of licenses via lottery every year. It's a fantastic time for hunters to try their luck because Vermont's moose population has been growing recently.

In Vermont, it is also legal to hunt black bears, although the state only issues a certain number of permits each year. The Vermont Fish & Wildlife Department has rigorous controls in place to guarantee the sustainability of the state's bear population, which is in good health.

It's crucial to obtain a hunting license in Vermont and adhere to all rules and regulations set forth by the government. Maps, rules, and safety advice are just a few of the services the Vermont Fish & Wildlife Department provides for hunters.

In Vermont, fishing and hunting are well-liked outdoor pursuits that provide participants the chance to take in the state's breathtaking scenery and diverse animals. Vermont offers a variety of options to explore your interest, regardless of your level of experience with fishing or hunting or your level of inexperience. To ensure a secure and sustainable experience, just be sure to obtain the required licenses and abide by all state laws.

CHAPTER EIGHT

Events & Festivals

The Vermont Maple Festival

Vermont is renowned for its unspoiled landscape, delectable maple syrup, and warm inhabitants. But many people might not be aware that the state also hosts a wide range of occasions and celebrations all throughout the year. The Vermont Maple Festival is one such event that is a must-see for any tourist in Vermont.

The little city of St. Albans in northwest Vermont hosts the Vermont Maple Festival every year. The festival honors Vermont's maple syrup industry, which is the biggest maple syrup producer in the country. The celebration usually takes place in late April, when the sap is flowing from the maple trees that have been tapped.

Since its inception in 1967, the festival has become an annual event in St. Albans and has increased in size and recognition. Today, it draws tens of thousands of tourists from around the globe who come to take advantage of the festival's offerings of maple syrup, food, crafts, and entertainment.

The maple syrup competition is one of the Vermont Maple Festival's key draws. Vermont's maple syrup producers from all across submit their best syrup for evaluation, and the festival is when the winners are revealed. The award-winning syrup, as well as other maple goods including maple cream, candies, and sugar, are available for sampling and purchase by visitors.

The Maple Exhibit Hall, where visitors may learn about the background and methodology of maple syrup production, is another well-liked festival event. The exhibit hall includes kid-friendly interactive games as well as displays and demonstrations on how maple syrup is manufactured.

The festival also has a wide range of food vendors selling everything from international cuisine to classic Vermont fare like maple donuts and maple cotton candy. While eating, guests can take in live music or one of the numerous shows that are taking place during the event.

The event hosts a Maple 5K run/walk for those who want to get some exercise. In addition to a t-shirt and a bottle of maple syrup, this event takes participants through the picturesque streets of St. Albans.

The Vermont Maple Festival is a fantastic place to get handmade goods and gifts. A sizable craft market selling homemade items including ceramics, jewelry, and apparel is a highlight of the festival. Additionally, visitors can buy Vermont-made goods like cheese, wine, and cider.

There is a Kid's Zone at the event where families with young children can take advantage of games and activities with a maple theme. Children can also enjoy the rides and the petting zoo.

The festival's Maple Parade, which happens on Saturday morning, is one of its highlights. There are floats, marching bands, and of course, displays with a maple theme in the parade. It's wonderful to see the neighborhood unite in support of the state's maple syrup business.

The Vermont Maple Festival is a wonderful way to enjoy St. Albans and the surrounding area's beauty and charm in addition to the events and activities. Visitors can go on a picturesque drive across

Vermont's undulating hills or go hiking in one of the numerous state parks.

Anyone traveling to Vermont in late April should not miss the Vermont Maple Festival. It's a celebration of the state's long history and stunning natural surroundings as well as a wonderful occasion to sample the state's renowned maple syrup in all its delectable varieties.

The Stowe Winter Carnival

Vermont is renowned for its pristine surroundings, breathtaking scenery, and year-round outdoor activities. However, Vermont is a well-liked travel destination for reasons other than its natural beauty. Additionally, Vermonters know how to have a good time, and the Stowe Winter Carnival is a prime illustration of that. Every January, the Stowe Winter Carnival is a yearly celebration that takes place in the center of Stowe, Vermont. The occasion celebrates winter and all the enjoyable activities that go along with it. The Stowe Winter Carnival will be thoroughly covered in this chapter, including its history, festivities, and everything you need to know to get the most out of your visit.

The Stowe Winter Carnival's past

To draw tourists to the town in the winter, the Stowe Winter Carnival was first held in 1921. The first carnival was a small event including ice skating, ski races, and other winter sports. The carnival's popularity increased over time, and new events were added to the calendar. The Stowe Winter Carnival is currently one of Vermont's largest winter events, drawing guests from all over the globe.

The Stowe Winter Carnival events

The week-long Stowe Winter Carnival offers a variety of activities for people of all ages. You can anticipate the following activities at the carnival:

Ice Carving Competition: The ice carving competition is one of the carnival's primary attractions. Professional ice carving teams from all over the world compete to build breathtaking ice works of art in the center of Stowe.

Playing volleyball on a court coated in the snow is part of the entertaining and unusual Snow Volleyball Tournament. Anyone who wants to take part in the tournament is welcome, and it's a great way to enjoy the wintertime outdoors.

The amusing Human Dog Sled Race comprises two-person teams racing around a track while towing a sled with a third team member on it. The problem? The team member pulling the sled is decked out as a dog!

Kids Carnival: The Kids Carnival at the Stowe Winter Carnival is a kid-focused event that is also a family-friendly affair. Face painting, games, and other entertaining activities are all part of this event.

Competitions for Ski and Snowboard: Stowe is renowned for its fantastic ski and snowboard terrain, and the carnival has a number of events for these sports. These events are must-sees for winter sports enthusiasts.

Snowshoe Race: The snowshoe race may be just what you're looking for if you're seeking a more low-key event. Anyone who wants to take part in this activity is welcome, and it's a wonderful way to discover the stunning winter scenery in the area of Stowe.

Live Performances: The Stowe Winter Carnival also honors music, and during the week, there are a number of live shows. There is something for everyone, whether you like rock, country, or blues.

Making Visit Plans

There are a few things to consider if you want to get the most out of your vacation to the Stowe Winter Carnival. The following advice can help you organize your trip:

Make Your Hotel Reservations Early: Since the Stowe Winter Carnival is a well-attended event, hotels and other lodgings may book up quickly. It's a good idea to make your reservations early to guarantee that you get the accommodations you want.

Don a Warm Coat: Vermont is in January, so the weather will be chilly. Wear warm clothing and the proper winter accessories, such as boots, gloves, and a hat.

Purchase in advance: It's a good idea to purchase your tickets in advance to avoid any last-minute headaches since several events at the carnival require them. The official Stowe Winter Carnival website has details about ticket availability and costs.

Verify the Calendar: It's a good idea to book your trip in advance because the Stowe Winter Carnival itinerary is jam-packed with activities. Choose the events you want to attend after looking over the calendar online.

Bring Cash: Although the majority of Stowe's merchants and establishments take credit cards, it's always a good idea to carry cash, particularly if you intend to attend events like the Kids Carnival or the ice carving competition where you might want to buy snacks or souvenirs.

There is a lot to see and do in the town of Stowe, even if the Stowe Winter Carnival festivities are the main draw. While you're here, spend some time checking out the town's shops, eateries, and other attractions.

The Stowe Winter Carnival is a distinctive and entertaining occasion that highlights all that is wonderful about Vermont's wintertime. There is something for everyone at the carnival, from ice carving competitions to snow volleyball games. The Stowe Snow Carnival is a must-see if you enjoy snow sports, live music, or are just looking for a fun family event. You now have all the knowledge necessary to organize your trip and make the most of your stay in Stowe thanks to this thorough guide. So get ready to enjoy the excitement and festivities of the Stowe Winter Carnival by packing your winter clothing.

The Vermont Brewers Festival

Vermont is renowned for its beautiful scenery, quaint towns, and burgeoning craft beer industry. The Vermont Brewers Festival, which takes place every summer, brings all of these components together for a weekend-long celebration of regional food, beer, and culture.

Since its beginning in 1991, the Vermont Brewers Festival has been a mainstay of the state's summer schedule. In the town of Burlington, it started as a modest meeting of local brewers and beer fans, but it has since expanded to become one of the biggest beer festivals in the nation.

On the shores of Lake Champlain near Burlington, the celebration lasts for two days in late July. More than 50 Vermont brewers will be represented, offering over 100 different beers, along with food vendors, live music, and a celebratory atmosphere that embodies Vermont's relaxed, welcoming way of life.

Here is everything you should know if you intend to attend the Vermont Brewers Festival so that you can enjoy yourself to the fullest.

Purchasing Tickets

Early in the spring is normally when tickets for the Vermont Brewers Festival go on sale, and they frequently sell out. It's crucial to mark your calendar if you plan to go and to be prepared to get tickets as soon as they go on sale.

There are a variety of ticket choices available, including Saturday or Sunday public admission tickets as well as VIP tickets that grant you early entry to the festival and a unique tasting glass. Prices vary based on the sort of ticket you buy and whether you buy them in advance or when it's closer to the festival.

Organizing Your Travel

There are several attractions in the vicinity that you can see if you're visiting Vermont for the Brewers Festival. Burlington is a thriving college town with an active downtown, fantastic restaurants, and a wide range of outdoor activities.

The Alchemist Brewery, Hill Farmstead Brewery, and Fiddlehead Brewing Company are just a few of the local breweries and brewpubs that are worth visiting. If you enjoy craft beer, you could easily spend a week visiting all of the local breweries and taprooms.

Plan ahead and reserve your lodging if you intend to remain in Burlington for the festival. Since the festival draws tens of thousands of visitors from across the nation, hotels and Airbnb rentals can quickly sell out.

Expectations for the Festival

Rain or shine, the Vermont Brewers Festival is a fun outdoor celebration. The festival area is situated on the shore of Lake Champlain, and attendees can anticipate a large number of beer tents, food stands, and live music performances throughout the day.

You'll get a tasting glass and a program with a list of all the brewers and beers that are available to try when you get to the festival. The festival grounds are yours to explore at your leisure, and you're welcome to try as many different beers as you desire (within reason, of course).

Live music is played all day long during the festival in addition to beer and food vendors. There are various stages set up across the festival grounds, and the music lineup often includes local and regional bands.

Steps to Have a Perfect Time at the Festival

Here are some pointers to assist first-timers get the most out of their experience at the Vermont Brewers Festival:

Keep Your Pace: With more than 100 different beers to try, it's simple to overindulge. Consider this a marathon rather than a race, and pace yourself properly. Take breaks between samples, drink plenty of water, and make sure you're eating enough food to metabolize all that beer.

It's crucial to have comfortable shoes that can handle rough terrain because the festival grounds are set up on grassy fields and gravel pathways. Make sure your footwear is up to the task because you'll be walking and standing a lot throughout the day.

Prepare Yourself: It's a good idea to arrive prepared for any potential weather since the festival is held rain or shine. If it's sunny, remember to pack sunscreen, a hat, and sunglasses.

If there is a chance of rain, pack a raincoat or an umbrella.

Take Breaks: The festival might be overwhelming at times because there is so much going on. Throughout the day, take breaks to relax, rejuvenate, and enjoy the scenery. To unwind and take in the scenery, find a shady area close to the lake. You may also browse some of the stalls selling crafts and mementos.

A terrific chance to sample new beers and learn about new brewers is the Vermont Brewers Festival. Never be scared to venture outside of your comfort zone and explore a new experience. Who knows, you might find a new beer you like!

For anybody who enjoys artisan beer, delectable food, and a fun atmosphere, the Vermont Brewers Festival is a must-attend event. It's a celebration of everything that makes Vermont unique, and it's a terrific chance to connect with other beer fans from throughout the nation.

If you intend to attend the festival, be sure to get your tickets in advance, make travel arrangements in advance, and be ready for a fun-filled day of entertainment and beer tasting. The most important thing is to enjoy yourself and drink responsibly.

The Vermont Balloon Festival

Vermont is a stunning state with a wide variety of tourist attractions and activities, from scenic landscapes and outdoor pursuits to cultural events and festivals. The Vermont Balloon Festival, one of the state's most well-liked occasions, draws tourists from all over the world. We will examine the background, high points, and attractions of the Vermont Balloon Festival in this chapter, giving you a thorough overview of this intriguing occasion.

The Vermont Balloon Festival's past

The 1970s marked the beginning of the Vermont Balloon Festival. The initial festival was held in 1979 in Stowe, Vermont, to raise money for the neighborhood hospital. Since then, the festival has developed into one of Vermont's most well-attended occasions, drawing thousands of tourists every year.

The event has been hosted at Quechee for the past 20 years after moving from Stowe, Killington, and other locales over the years. The Quechee Polo Grounds, where the celebration is now hosted, has plenty of room for balloons to launch and land.

Vermont Balloon Festival highlights

Every year in June, a four-day event called the Vermont Balloon Festival takes place. For attendees of all ages, the festival offers a wide range of events and attractions, including:

Launching balloons

The balloon launches are of course the festival's main attraction. From the Quechee Polo Grounds, more than 20 hot air balloons launch daily, painting the sky with a kaleidoscope of hues. Visitors may watch the balloons launch and soar in the air, and for a price, they can even go for a ride in one of the balloons.

Glowing Balloons

The festival also includes a Balloon Glow, which happens on Saturday night, in addition to the launches. The balloons are lit up and tied to the ground during the Balloon Glow, producing an amazing visual display.

Craft Show

The festival also includes a craft fair where regional makers and retailers offer a selection of unique handmade goods, gifts, and souvenirs.

Visitors can look around the booths and purchase distinctive Vermont-made goods.

food and beverage

The festival also provides a variety of food and beverage options, from regional delicacies like maple syrup and Vermont cheddar cheese to traditional festival fares like funnel cakes and fried dough. Wines and artisan brews made in Vermont are also available to visitors.

The Festival's Nearby Attractions

Although there are many other sights and activities in the area, the Vermont Balloon Festival is unquestionably the main draw. A few well-liked sights close to the festival are:

Toquee Gorge

Only a few miles from the festival grounds is the stunning natural wonder known as the Quechee Gorge. For a closer look, visitors can climb down to the canyon's floor. It is a deep cleft that the Ottauquechee River formed.

Natural Science Institute of Vermont

A wildlife rehabilitation facility and nature center can be found in Quechee at the Vermont Institute of Natural Sciences. Visitors can view several raptors, such as eagles and hawks, and discover Vermont's natural heritage.

Glassblowing by Simon Pearce

Simon Pearce is a well-known glassblower who creates exquisite lighting and glassware. In the Quechee workshop, visitors can observe the glassblowers at work and browse the retail space for one-of-a-kind items.

Every traveler should put the Vermont Balloon Festival on their bucket list since it is an exceptional and unforgettable occasion. The Vermont Balloon Festival has plenty to offer everyone, whether you're a seasoned festival-goer or just seeking a fun and family-friendly weekend escape. There is a lot to see and do at the event, from the stunning balloon launches and Balloon Glow to the craft fair and food sellers. The Quechee Gorge and the Vermont Institute of Natural Science are just a couple of the surrounding attractions that allow guests to extend their trip over an entire weekend.

The Vermont Antique & Classic Car Meet

The Vermont Antique and Classic Car Meet is among the most thrilling occasions that take place in Vermont. This annual celebration of vintage and classic vehicles is held in Stowe, Vermont. The gathering of car enthusiasts from across the nation allows them to share their passion for classic cars and show off their stunning rides.

The Vermont Antique and Classic Car Meet's past

Since its founding in 1957, the Vermont Antique & Classic Car Meet has a long and illustrious history. A group of antique car enthusiasts who wished to establish a venue for showing their cherished vehicles founded the event. A few aficionados attended the first meet, which was held in the tiny Vermont town of Waterbury. The event has gained popularity over the years and now draws thousands of vehicle aficionados from throughout the nation.

Today, Stowe, Vermont hosts the Vermont Antique and Classic Car Meet, which has grown to be one of the most significant occasions in the state. The Vermont Vehicle Enthusiasts (VAE), a non-profit group devoted to preserving the history of the vehicle and promoting its status in Vermont's culture, is in charge of organizing the event.

The Vermont Antique and Classic Car Meet: What to expect

In Stowe, Vermont, there is a three-day event called the Vermont Antique and Classic Car Meet. Every year in August, the event draws a sizable number of auto aficionados from throughout the nation. Visitors can anticipate seeing a wide variety of vintage and classic cars on show at the open event.

The vehicle parade, which happens on the first day of the event, is one of its highlights. The procession, which is a sight to behold, includes hundreds of vintage and classic vehicles. A large variety of automobiles, including vintage, classic, muscle, and sports cars, will be on exhibit for visitors to admire. There are also several other unique exhibits, such as displays of race cars and military vehicles.

Visitors can anticipate seeing a variety of merchants providing automobile-related goods and services in addition to cars. Additionally, there are food stands selling a variety of delectable treats like local cheese, homemade ice cream, and Vermont maple syrup.

There are other educational activities that take place during the event for individuals who want to learn more about old and classic cars. These occasions include lectures on auto repair, auto history, and auto maintenance.

The Vermont Antique and Classic Car Meet attending advice

There are a few things you should keep in mind if you intend to attend the Vermont Antique and Classic Car Meet. First, make sure you are dressed for the weather. Be cautious to dress in light, breathable clothing in August because Vermont may get rather hot and muggy.

Second, don't forget to pack a camera. You should take advantage of the many opportunities to take pictures of the stunning cars that are being displayed.

Third, make sure you get there early. There may be a parking shortage due to the event's big attendance. You will have a greater chance of getting a nice parking spot and avoiding the throng if you arrive early.

Finally, make sure to benefit from all the educational activities that are offered throughout the event. These events will improve your overall event experience and provide a fantastic opportunity to learn more about vintage and classic vehicles.

The thrilling Vermont Antique & Classic Car Meet honors the heritage and culture of the automobile. The gathering of car enthusiasts from across the nation allows them to share their passion for classic cars and show off their stunning rides. The Vermont Antique and Classic Car Meet is a must-see event if you love cars or are just seeking for a fun and different experience in Vermont. This event will enthrall visitors of all ages thanks to its stunning location in Stowe and the huge variety of cars on exhibit.

CHAPTER NINE

Basic Info for Tourist

Currency, Language & Time Zone

The fundamentals of currency, language, and time zone should all be taken into account while making travel plans to Vermont. You may travel with ease and prevent any unpleasant shocks if you are aware of these essential facts.

Currency

The US dollar (USD) is Vermont's designated official currency. Like the rest of the country, Vermont employs a decimal system in which one dollar is equivalent to 100 cents. One cent (penny), five cents (nickel), ten cents (dime), twenty-five cents (quarter), and one dollar (Sacagawea or Presidential dollar) are the coin denominations that are offered. There are one, two, five, ten, twenty, fifty, and one hundred dollar bills available.

In Vermont, the majority of establishments, including hotels, eateries, and retail stores, accept credit and debit cards. Additionally, most towns and cities have ATMs for quick access to cash. However, it's always advisable to keep some cash on hand for smaller purchases.

Language

English is the most extensively used language in Vermont and is also the state's official language. However, some people in Vermont also speak French as a result of the state's proximity to Canada and French heritage. Increasingly more locals and visitors are fluent in Spanish.

It's a good idea to learn some fundamental English words if you're visiting Vermont from a country where English isn't spoken to help you get around. Since most Vermonters are friendly and accommodating, they'll probably be happy to help you if you're having trouble speaking English.

Hour Zone

The Eastern Time Zone (ET), which is five hours behind Coordinated Universal Time (UTC-5), is where Vermont is situated. When daylight saving time is in force, which begins on the second

Sunday in March and ends on the first Sunday in November, Vermont is four hours behind UTC (UTC-4) in time.

There are four states in the US that do not observe daylight saving time, and Vermont is one of them. This indicates that Vermont is in the same time zone as New York and Boston during the summer, but that Montreal and Toronto are in the same time zone as Vermont during the winter.

It's crucial to arrange your schedule well if you are coming to Vermont from a different time zone to prevent confusion. As soon as you arrive, make sure to set your watch and other electronics to the local time zone.

Vermont is a stunning state with a vibrant cultural history and friendly people. To make your trip as smooth and pleasurable as possible, be sure to keep some important considerations regarding currency, language, and time zone in mind as you plan your travels. Vermont has something to offer everyone, whether you're coming for the first time or coming back for another experience.

Safety Tips & Emergency Services

Visitors may enjoy a range of sights and outdoor activities in the lovely state of Vermont. Despite the fact that it is generally a secure area to go to, it is still vital to be aware of potential risks and be prepared for emergencies. Important safety advice and details about Vermont's emergency services are provided in this chapter.

Tips for General Safety

Pay attention to your surroundings: Always be mindful of your surroundings, whether you're strolling through the city or through the woods. This necessitates being aware of the people and vehicles in your immediate vicinity as well as any potential dangers like rocky terrain or slick surfaces.

lug a phone around: It's essential to have a method of calling for assistance in case of an emergency. In case you need to recharge, make sure your phone is completely charged and that you have a charger on hand.

obey the guidelines: To ensure the safety of tourists, Vermont has a number of laws and regulations in place, including traffic laws and trail regulations. To prevent mishaps or fines, make sure you are aware of these regulations and adhere to them.

Keep an eye out for wildlife: bears, moose, and snakes can all be found in Vermont. Know the possible dangers and how to respond if you come across wildlife.

Be ready for the weather: Since Vermont's climate is changeable, it's necessary to be ready for any eventualities. Before going outside, make sure you are dressed appropriately for the season and have the necessary equipment.

Crisis Services

There are numerous resources available to assist you in Vermont if you find yourself in an emergency circumstance.

911: Call 911 to access emergency services in case of an emergency. You can call this number to report mishaps, fires, medical emergencies, and other circumstances that demand quick action.

Hospitals: The state of Vermont is home to a number of hospitals and healthcare facilities. The University of Vermont Medical Center in Burlington, Rutland Regional Medical Center in Rutland, and Southwestern Vermont Medical Center in Bennington are a few of the larger hospitals.

Police: The state of Vermont's law enforcement is handled by the Vermont State Police. Numerous communities and cities also have their own different police forces. Calling 911 or your local department's non-emergency number can put you in touch with the police if you need to report a crime or make a help request.

Fire departments: The municipalities in Vermont are served by a number of volunteer and professional fire departments that offer fire and emergency services. Call 911 or your local department's non-emergency number if you need to report a fire or other emergency.

There are several search and rescue teams who can assist you if you become lost or hurt while hiking or exploring Vermont's wilderness areas. The Vermont Department of Public Safety oversees these squads, which are frequently comprised of volunteers.

Poison control: The Vermont Poison Center can provide aid if you or someone you know consumes a potentially dangerous substance. You can easily contact the center at 1-800-222-1222.

Roadside assistance: There are several services that can assist you if your car breaks down or you have a flat tire while traveling in Vermont. A couple of the biggest suppliers are Allstate Motor Club and AAA.

Natural catastrophes

Visitors visiting Vermont should be aware of the hazards and how to prepare for them. Natural disasters can strike anywhere, even Vermont.

Flooding: Rivers and streams in Vermont are prone to overflowing during the spring and early summer when the snow melts and strong rainfall might occur. Be mindful of the possibility of flooding if you're traveling during these times, and pay attention to any flood warnings or advisories that may be issued by local authorities. If you live in a flood-prone location, be prepared to leave if required.

Storms, tornadoes, and even hurricanes are among the severe weather events that Vermont may experience. Check the weather forecast frequently if you're traveling during a stormy season, and be ready to seek shelter if required.

Earthquakes: Although they don't happen as frequently as other natural disasters, earthquakes can occur in Vermont. When you sense an earthquake, find a safe place to hide and remain inside until the shaking stops. Be prepared to take cover once more if required because aftershocks can happen.

Winter storms: Although Vermont is renowned for having snowy winters, a lot of snow and ice may sometimes cause hazardous situations like power outages and blocked highways. Make sure you have the right clothing and equipment for the weather if you're traveling in the winter, and be ready for delays or power outages.

Visitors should be mindful of potential health dangers in Vermont in addition to probable natural calamities. For instance, Vermont has a high prevalence of Lyme disease because of the abundance of deer ticks there. Wear long sleeves and pants, use insect repellent, and check yourself and your pets for ticks if you intend to spend time outside.

Although traveling in Vermont is generally safe, it's important to be aware of any risks and to be prepared for emergencies. You can make sure that your visit to Vermont is safe and enjoyable by paying attention to these safety recommendations and being ready for emergencies. Always be mindful of your surroundings, keep a phone with you, and be ready for inclement weather and potential natural calamities. You may travel to Vermont safely and with fond memories if you keep these safety measures in mind.

Health & Medical Service

It's crucial to have a strategy in place for any unforeseen medical requirements when traveling. Vermont offers a range of options for residents and visitors alike, whether you require urgent care, routine medical services, or simply a prescription refill.

Hospitals and medical facilities: The state of Vermont is home to a number of hospitals and healthcare facilities. These hospitals offer a range of medical services, including inpatient and outpatient treatment as well as emergency services.

The major hospital in Vermont and the academic medical hub of the area is the University of Vermont Medical Center (UVM Medical Center), which is situated in Burlington. The hospital provides a wide spectrum of medical services, such as neurology, cancer treatment, women's health, and emergency care.

Central Vermont Medical Center is a non-profit community hospital with a location in Berlin that provides a variety of medical services, such as emergency care, surgery, and diagnostic imaging.

Southwestern Vermont Medical Center is a community hospital with a number of medical services available, including emergency treatment, inpatient care, and outpatient care. It is situated in Bennington.

Gifford Medical Center is a non-profit hospital with a location in Randolph that provides a range of medical services, such as emergency care, family medicine, and behavioral health.

Rutland Regional Medical Center is a community hospital that offers a range of medical services, such as emergency care, cancer treatment, and orthopedic services. It is situated in Rutland.

Urgent care facilities: These facilities offer non-life-threatening illnesses and injuries rapid medical attention. Usually accessible after regular business hours, these facilities don't require an appointment.

Burlington, Rutland, and St. Albans are just a few of the facilities that ClearChoiceMD Urgent Care provides throughout Vermont. Treatment for illnesses, accidents, and other medical disorders is among the range of medical services offered by urgent care facilities.

Northshire Medical Center: This Manchester-based facility offers primary care, specialized care, urgent care, and other medical services.

Community health centers: These facilities offer healthcare to people and families who might not have access to more regular healthcare settings. Primary care, dental care, and behavioral health services are just a few of the medical services provided by these establishments.

Community Health Centers of Burlington: With facilities all across the city, Community Health Centers of Burlington offers a range of medical services, such as primary care, dental care, and behavioral health services.

The Northeast Kingdom is served by Northern Counties Health Care, which is based in St. Johnsbury and offers primary care, dental care, and behavioral health services to individuals and families.

Springfield Medical Care Systems: Based in Springfield, this organization offers primary care, dental care, and behavioral health services to people and families in southern Vermont.

Pharmacy: Pharmacies sell over-the-counter medicines, prescription drugs, and other medical supplies. Additionally, many pharmacies provide vaccinations, flu shots, and other preventive healthcare services.

CVS Pharmacy sells prescription drugs, over-the-counter medicines, and other medical supplies at a number of sites throughout Vermont.

Walgreens Pharmacy: With multiple sites across Vermont, Walgreens Pharmacy offers prescription drugs, over-the-counter drugs, and other medical supplies.

Rite Aid Pharmacy sells prescription drugs, over-the-counter medicines, and other medical supplies at a number of sites throughout Vermont.

Both residents and tourists in Vermont have access to a range of healthcare alternatives. There are many facilities that offer medical services throughout the state, including hospitals, medical centers, urgent care clinics, and community health centers. Additionally, pharmacies offer prescription medicines, over-the-counter medicines, and other medical supplies, making it simple for travelers to buy what they need or refill their prescriptions.

State's Parks & Recreation Areas

State parks and recreational areas in Vermont are some of the best sites to explore the state's famed natural beauty. Vermont's state parks have something to offer everyone, from the majestic Green Mountains to the serene shores of Lake Champlain. We'll examine some of Vermont's greatest state parks and recreational sites in this section, emphasizing their distinctive qualities and draws.

Park Smugglers' Notch State

Smugglers' Notch State Park, which is situated in the center of the Green Mountains, is a well-liked spot for hikers, rock climbers, and nature lovers. The park is named for the congested mountain route that previously served as smugglers' main route for moving goods between Vermont and Canada. Today, visitors can hike the park's challenging trails, which provide breathtaking views of the mountains and valleys nearby.

The Sterling Pond Trail, which leads to a beautiful alpine lake, is one of the park's most well-liked hikes. A little more than two miles long, the trail leads walkers through a variety of environments, from thick forests to rocky outcrops. The park's sheer cliffs that surround the Notch offer a variety of difficult routes for rock climbers to choose from.

Smugglers' Notch State Park provides camping, fishing, and swimming along with hiking and rock climbing. The park offers a day-use area with a beach and picnic tables, as well as 20 tent/RV sites and 14 lean-tos.

State Park at Lake Carmi

Due to its crystal-clear waters and plethora of fish, Lake Carmi State Park is a well-liked location for boaters and anglers. One of Vermont's largest inland bodies of water, the lake has a surface area of more than 1,400 acres. Visitors can bring their own boats to launch from the park's boat ramp or rent kayaks, canoes, and paddleboards from the facility.

At Lake Carmi State Park, fishing is another well-liked activity. Anglers frequently catch bass, northern pike, and yellow perch. The park features a fishing dock, a fish cleaning station, and a nature center with educational activities about the lake's ecosystem.

There are several hiking routes in Lake Carmi State Park that wind through the park's wetlands and forests for those who would rather stay on dry land. There is a chance to see animals along the paths, including beavers, otters, and great blue herons.

State Park of Mount Ascutney

Southern Vermont's Mount Ascutney State Park is home to some of the state's outstanding views.

Over 3,000 feet above sea level, the park's namesake peak offers panoramic views of the surrounding landscape. The Weathersfield Trail offers a six-mile roundtrip climb to the peak that takes around four hours to accomplish.

Mountain biking, equestrian riding, and camping are also available in Mount Ascutney State Park in addition to hiking. Mountain bikers and equestrian riders can use the park's network of trails, and there are 39 campsites for overnight stays.

State Park near Butte Bay

On the shores of Lake Champlain, Button Bay State Park is a well-liked spot for picnicking, swimming, and boating. A big sandy beach, a designated swimming area, a boat launch, and docks are all present in the park.

Button Bay State Park offers a variety of hiking trails with breathtaking views of the lake and the Adirondack Mountains in addition to water sports. The nature center of the park offers classes about the environment of the lake and the background of the region.

State Park Emerald Lake

A hidden gem tucked away in the southern Green Mountains is Emerald Lake State Park. The park's crystal-clear, emerald-green waters, which are supplied by a local stream, gave rise to its name. The lake is a well-liked location for boating, swimming, and fishing. Rainbow and brown trout can be caught in the lake's waters.

A system of hiking routes circles the lake and winds through the park's woodlands. There is a chance to see animals on the paths, including deer, moose, and black bears. The park has a boat launch and a number of kayaks, canoes, and paddleboards for rent for those who like to stay on the water.

Park State of Jamaica

Southern Vermont's Jamaica State Park is renowned for its beautiful swimming holes and waterfalls. The Ball Mountain Dam, which was constructed in the park in the 1950s to reduce local flooding, is located there. Swimming and sunbathing enthusiasts enjoy the numerous pools and waterfalls that the dam's construction resulted in.

A network of hiking paths in the park also provides access to Ball Mountain's summit, where you can enjoy breathtaking views of the surrounding valleys. The park features a designated fishing area as well as a picnic spot for those who would rather stay near the water.

State Forest of Groton

With more than 26,000 acres of forests, lakes, and mountains to explore, Groton State Forest is one of Vermont's largest state parks. Five different lakes make up the park, and each one has its own special features and activities.

The main lake in the park, Lake Groton, is a well-liked spot for boating, fishing, and swimming. The lake offers a boat launch and docks for boaters, as well as a sandy beach and a designated bathing area.

A smaller, more secluded lake called Seyon Pond is well-liked by anglers. The pond features a fishing dock and a cleaning station, and it is stocked with trout.

The Groton State Forest includes a number of hiking routes that wind through its woodlands and around its lakes in addition to its lakes. There are more than 200 campsites spread out over the park, which also provides camping.

Visitors can get a close-up look at Vermont's natural splendor at one of the state parks and recreational sites. Vermont's state parks have plenty to offer, whether you're searching for a strenuous hike, a breathtaking drive, or a quiet place to unwind. The state parks of Vermont are a must-see for everyone traveling to the state, from the majestic heights of the Green Mountains to the serene shores of Lake Champlain.

Final Thoughts

It is difficult to find a state in the United States that has a similar combination of historical significance, cultural diversity, and natural beauty as Vermont. Vermont is a place that should be on every traveler's bucket list, from the breathtaking views of the Green Mountains to the cozy charm of its little communities. We'll discuss our final observations and travel tips for Vermont in this chapter.

Vermont Travelling

Since Vermont is a small state, getting around is not too difficult. Several airports, including Vermont's largest airport, Burlington International Airport, serve the state. Vermont can also be reached by train, bus, or automobile. To properly experience Vermont after you arrive, we advise hiring a car. A lot of Vermont's picturesque roads are enjoyable to travel, especially in the fall when the leaves are changing color.

Vermont Travel Season

Every season in Vermont provides something different, making it a year-round vacation destination. When Vermont's ski resorts are open, between December and March, you should travel there if you enjoy winter sports. The best seasons for outdoor pursuits like hiking, riding, and kayaking are spring and summer. Vermont's most favored season is fall and with good reason. The state's numerous apple orchards and pumpkin patches are bustling with activity, and the fall color is simply magnificent.

Vermont lodging options

Vermont has a wide range of lodging choices, from opulent resorts to inviting bed and breakfasts. Consider booking a room at one of Vermont's numerous historic inns or guesthouses if you want a genuinely one-of-a-kind experience. These buildings, several of which are on the National Register of Historic Places, provide a window into Vermont's illustrious past. There are several low-cost hotels and motels available in the state if you're on a tight budget.

Activities in Vermont

From recreational activities to cultural experiences, Vermont has something to offer everyone. Some of our top suggestions for things to do in Vermont are listed below:

Discover the small towns of Vermont: There are numerous quaint tiny villages in Vermont, each with its own distinct personality. Visit the charming boutiques in Manchester, stroll through Woodstock's ancient streets, or take a lovely drive through the Mad River Valley.

Go snowboarding or skiing: There is a solid reason why Vermont is well known for its ski resorts. Vermont's ski resorts cater to skiers and snowboarders of all skill levels, offering everything from the kid-friendly slopes of Okemo Mountain Resort to the demanding terrain of Stowe Mountain Resort.

Visit the Ben & Jerry's Ice Cream Factory: Visit the Waterbury, Vermont, location of the Ben & Jerry's Ice Cream Factory. You may try some of the varieties and get a behind-the-scenes look at how the company creates its well-known ice cream.

Hike the Long Trail: Vermont's 272-mile-long Long Trail is a popular hiking route. It's the country's first long-distance hiking trail and features some of the state's most breathtaking panoramas.

Discover Burlington: The largest city in Vermont, Burlington offers a variety of urban and outdoor experiences. Visit the renowned Fleming Museum of Art, take a boat ride on Lake Champlain, or stroll through the pedestrian-friendly Church Street Marketplace.

Try some Vermont craft beer: Vermont is home to many craft brewers, including The Alchemist Brewery and the renowned Hill Farmstead Brewery. Visit a brewery and try some of the greatest craft beer Vermont has to offer.

Every traveler's must-see list should include Vermont. Vermont has much to offer, whether you're seeking outdoor activities, cultural encounters, or just a quiet break. From the Green Mountains' breathtaking views to its little towns' charming atmosphere

Made in the USA
Middletown, DE
27 June 2023

33826259R00124